This book is an inspiring and empo................................. ...... of military spouse life, showcasing the remarkable resilience and dedication of these often unsung heroes. Beautifully and thoughtfully written by the insightful Jen McDonald, this captivating narrative illuminates the challenges and triumphs faced by military spouses, offering a profound glimpse into a life of constant change.

I highly recommend this book to anyone who is looking for a brighter light to help them navigate the world as we know it. —**Trevor Romain**, bestselling author, speaker, and co-founder of *The Comfort Crew for Military Kids*

This is a wonderful read and masterfully captures countless emotions and challenges faced by military spouses every day. The life lessons she shares will be valuable whether a new military spouse, a retired military spouse, or the military member. The multigenerational stories touch the heart and highlight the incredible gift our military spouses are to our nation. —**Brooke McLean**, CMSgt, USAF (Retired) and President and CEO of the Air Force Enlisted Village

Truly a great resource for new and seasoned spouses alike. I could hardly put this book down. I found myself chuckling and crying at times. So much to be gained from these experiences! Educational, entertaining, informative, insightful, and inspiring are just a few words I would use to describe this book. It is truly worth using and sharing! —**Mrs. Paula Roy**, Spouse of the 16th Chief Master Sergeant of the Air Force (Retired)

Milspouse Matters is a must-read for all and a glorious depiction of the strength of military spouses. Jen is a master of words as she shares the beautiful ebbs and flows of military life; from love and loss, strength and weakness, victory marches and dark trenches, and the joy that shines through every moment. I've watched Jen's journey unfold over many years, and she is an inspiration to everyone who lays their eyes across her pages. You'll laugh, you'll cry, and you won't be able to put it down until the last word. —**Kariah Manwaring**, *Military Spouse Magazine*

"You knew what you signed up for." The first sentence in Jen McDonald's book, *Milspouse Matters*, makes it clear that this book is for us. By us, I mean those of us who have married the military and all the challenges it entails. Jen shares her personal stories and also includes a great cross section of others' experiences. The encouragement and support is woven throughout as she shares a wide spectrum of experiences, even those that are difficult. If you are a military spouse, you need this book tucked into your nightstand for those moments when you need some reassurance that you can power through the next challenge or deployment. I'll be recommending it to all my military parent and spouse friends. —**Elaine Brye**, author of *Be Safe, Love Mom: A Military Mom's Stories of Courage, Comfort, and Surviving Life on the Homefront*

In this wide-ranging collection of stories, Jen mines the deep experiences of her own life and honest conversations with military spouses to discover gems of meaning and mentorship. As a fellow military spouse and editor, it's been my joy to work with Jen on this book. Her shining messages of hope and encouragement will make a difference to every reader. —**Terri Barnes**, editor, *Stars and Stripes* columnist, and author of *Spouse Calls: Messages from a Military Life*

A sweet slice of military life, full of encouragement and military spouse can-do attitude. These stories of love, faith, joy, and heartache will resonate whether you're a brand new spouse, have a few moves under your belt, or supporting a loved one. Thank you, Jen, for a journey of laughter and tears. —**Kate Horrell**, Navy spouse (Retired) and Founder, Kings High Media

This book puts the "REAL" in the real life lived by less than 1% of America. From the small victories of changing out car batteries to mastering acronyms and making a will at age 22, Jen taps into the unique and ordinary moments that make the military world a special place to live. From zip code amnesia and starting a marriage on two different continents to overseas living and the conundrum of having too many curtains, this is a "non Hallmark" glimpse into our Milspouse world. —**Kathleen Palmer**, *Mission:Milspouse* Director of Content, and Army Spouse of 27 years

Jen McDonald's book is a delightful gift of stories that needed to be told. As a fellow military spouse, I laughed, cringed, and nodded in sympathetic commiseration as I read both her stories and the stories she shared from other military spouses across the generations. *Milspouse Matters*, a book that celebrates resilience, is the perfect read for those just entering the military world, those who've been part of it for a while, and also for civilians who would like to understand our military lifestyle better. —**Julie Tully**, author of *Dispatches From The Cowgirl: Through The Looking Glass With A Navy Diplomat's Wife*

A must-read for spouses at any point in their service member's military career! If you've been "married to the military," at any point, these stories are a great reminder that you are not alone. *Milspouse Matters* also makes a great gift for friends or family members who tell you that you "knew what you signed up for!" —**Stephanie Montague**, Army spouse (Retired), Founder of *Poppin' Smoke*

Through a collection of carefully selected stories, Jen McDonald, author of *Milspouse Matters*, has written a love letter to the life of a military spouse. For years, I went through life as a military spouse feeling like I was the only one unable to keep up with the acronyms, having a hard time accepting that I was now a *dependent*, and fighting a hopeless battle against the concept that the mission must always come first. That sense of belonging is a priceless gift that only a military spouse like the author, who never gave up no matter how hard the challenge, could have given the rest of us. —**Brunella Costagliola**, Owner of *The Military Editor®Agency*

MILSPOUSE MATTERS

MILSPOUSE MATTERS

Sharing Strength
Through Our Stories

JEN MCDONALD

W. Brand Publishing
NASHVILLE, TENNESSEE

j.brand@wbrandpub.com
W. Brand Publishing
www.wbrandpub.com

Cover design: designchik.net
Cover imagery: Publisher's personal photo collection,
    MilStock, Shutterstock

Editor: Terri Barnes
Copy Editor: Virginia Bhashkar

Milspouse Matters —1st ed.

Available in Hardcover, Paperback, Kindle, and eBook formats.

Hardcover: 978-1-956906-65-3
Paperback: 978-1-956906-66-0
eBook: 978-1-956906-67-7
Library of Congress Control Number: 2023916894

TABLE OF CONTENTS

DISCLAIMER

The events written about in this book are as remembered and recorded by the author, who kept journals and a private blog for her family through the years mentioned, as well as from interviews conducted with military spouses from the Bob Hope Village and the *Milspouse Matters* podcast. Some names have been changed for privacy purposes. This content is neither endorsed by nor affiliated with the U.S. Department of Defense, any of its service branches, the U.S. Department of Veterans Affairs, or any U.S. government agency.

Some content was previously published in *Military Spouse* magazine and the author's first book, *You Are Not Alone: Encouragement for the Heart of a Military Spouse* (Little Things Press, 2016), as well as on MilitaryByOwner.com and Jen's website, jen-mcdonald.com. Used with permission.

DEDICATION

To military spouses everywhere, past and present: You inspire me every day. Never forget: You are brave, you are strong, and you've got this.

To my dear Steve: You're the reason I went on this adventure called military life. I've come to realize over the years what an example you've been to me of the ability to maintain a positive attitude and *joie de vivre* while going through challenges and the dailiness of regular life. Whether by inviting me to walk along the harbor behind our house in Hawaii at sunset and "feed the fish" or blaring Family Force 5 through the minivan's speakers for the kids on a road trip, your ability to throw yourself wholeheartedly into enjoying a moment has always been something of a wonder to me. I'll never forget how you'd say something like, "This will make such a great story one day!" or, "Can you believe we get to live through this?" in the midst of a natural disaster or when PCS orders got changed at the last minute. It's not natural for me to approach life this way, but I'm learning from you. Thank you for always supporting and believing in me. You mean everything to me.

INTRODUCTION

Take one young girl from New Mexico (me), a handsome young airman from Georgia (my husband, Steve), add equal parts love and naivete, and you have the ingredients for what would concoct a grand adventure of thirty-one years of military life. Looking back now, a few years after military retirement, I have no regrets. I've had opportunities for growth, adventure, and finding confidence and independence on the wild ride that has been my life as a military spouse. I've had small triumphs, like following a YouTube tutorial to switch out a car battery by myself in an icy garage, and major victories, like surviving Steve's year-long deployment while we were stationed overseas. These and many other experiences shaped who I am today. While stationed both stateside and overseas, our family visited bucket-list destinations on several continents. We learned to appreciate our little family unit at each new location when all we had was each other. We made precious friends who remain in our lives to this day.

Each military family has their own stories—sometimes thrilling, sometimes funny, sometimes harrowing. As a military spouse, I find strength, connection, and reassurance in the stories of others in military life. As a freelance writer and podcaster, I've spent years discovering and sharing stories in the military community. Whether I'm telling my own stories or passing along someone else's, my goal is always to encourage and uplift. To share a story is to share the power it conveys.

I published my first book, *You Are Not Alone: Encouragement for the Heart of a Miliary Spouse*, in 2016 and later launched the *Milspouse Matters* podcast to support and provide resources for the amazing group of people who will have my heart forever.

As part of the work I do, I had the opportunity to visit the Bob Hope Village, an independent living community for Air Force widows in Shalimar, Florida. I interviewed some of the residents and discovered another generation of inspiring women with stories to match. At first glance, the Bob Hope Village seems like any retirement community, with its chapel, community center, cafeteria, and modern apartments. But there's a difference, a military sensibility. The women I talked to there were all widows whose husbands served during the wars of the twentieth century: World War II, the Korean War, the Vietnam War. When they were young military wives, there wasn't as much military family support as we have today. They had to figure out a lot on their own, yet they survived and thrived as military spouses.

They told me about the wrenching separations from their husbands again and again as they were shipped off to war, not knowing when or even if they'd hear from them again. With no email, no video chat, no text messaging, they were lucky to get a letter every few weeks. They often coped alone with the fallout of war and its effects on their husbands and families. Like us, they uprooted their families every few years. One woman told me about a cross-country move in the 1960s, reminiscing about how her family had lived in their station-wagon. She and her husband took turns sleeping on the ground while their little ones rested on a crib mattress in the back of the car. She told the story as if it was an adventure and not an inconvenience.

The stories from past generations and those I hear from modern-day military spouses on my podcast reveal that while much has changed for military families, so much more remains the same. We still experience deployments, moves, fear, constant change, and the need to adjust to military culture and embrace the unknown. We also share positive experiences: adventure, travel, strong family bonds, and wonderful memories.

The stories I heard at Bob Hope Village mirrored the experiences of the men and women I speak to today, as well as my own. We all have tales of adventure, grit, hope, and strength, stories well worth telling and re-telling. I am forever grateful to all the spouses who were willing to share their stories with me and allow me to share them with you.

So, whether you're a new or very seasoned (even salty) military spouse, a family member or friend hoping to better understand the nuances of military life, or just someone who loves to hear other people's stories, my hope is that here you'll find comfort and strength for your own unique journey.

Every story matters.

Blessings,

Jen McDonald

PART 1

LOVE STORIES

CHOOSING LOVE, FINDING STRENGTH

I choose you and I'll choose you over and over. Without pause, without a doubt, in a heartbeat, I will keep choosing you.
—Kiersten White

"You knew what you signed up for."

If you're a military spouse, you've probably heard this phrase. These words may be implied or uttered thoughtlessly when you express your weariness with the everyday frustrations of military life. You may be worrying about finding a job, watching your kids adjust to yet another new home and school, trying to make connections at your latest duty station, or feeling the emotional distance when your marriage takes second place to the military mission. In all these situations, we often get the same message: "Suck it up, Buttercup. You chose this life."

You may feel as if there's another entity in your marriage, and yes, that's the way it is while your spouse serves their country. It's not just the two of you anymore. Now, there are three of you with competing interests: the one you love, you, and the military.

Did you really know what you signed up for?

I sure didn't. I had a vague sense of duty to country, of course, but I didn't foresee giving up literal years of time with my husband, or constantly reinventing myself as we moved back and forth across the world. Could I have imagined how this life would stretch me both emotionally and physically?

Did I envision the lonely nights, the tears I'd choke back as I sat alone yet again at our children's recitals or baseball games, the ache of missing home? Was there any way I could have known ahead of time the toll military life would take on our marriage? That there would be moments when I wasn't sure we would make it? No, I didn't know what I signed up for, and I'm thankful I didn't. If I had, I might have given up before I started, and I would have missed out on the many positive experiences of military life.

I fell in love with a man who happened to be in the military. Does anyone really know, when falling in love, exactly what they are signing up for? I doubt it, so I don't expect military spouses to automatically know what military life will be or what it will cost. What I did know was that I chose Steve. I still choose him and that's what matters, then and now. Back then I figured I could handle whatever that choice entailed. I was mostly right, but some days (months, years) have been much harder than I expected.

For all it costs, the military life I chose to share with my husband also has rewards. Usually not so much in dollars and cents, but in things money can't buy: rich relationships and priceless experiences.

BELONGING AND IDENTITY

As a preteen and teenager, I insisted that I could not wait to get away from my hometown. I wanted to live, walk to the community pool, or go to a store without running into someone who knew me or my family. They'd pin me down, these well-meaning, often older folks.

"Oh, look! Little Jennifer Brown! How you've grown!"

I'd groan inwardly through the required small talk, because I was raised to be polite—and trust me, it would get back to my parents if I wasn't. I'd listen to the updates about people I barely knew, answer questions about how my parents or grandparents were doing, hear the rehashing of something funny or embarrassing I'd done when I was little that I would apparently never live down. Forcing a smile, I'd try to move on quickly. Oh, how these experiences annoyed me as an awkward teenager trying to carve out her own identity in the shadow of a well-loved and very friendly family.

I soon learned as a military spouse how much I missed the comfort of being known. Just a few years later, I could only wish my errands would be interrupted by running into someone I knew—someone who knew me—*anyone*. I'd also realize as a military dependent that people didn't have much interest in who my parents were, any of my personal information, or even my first name. I noticed it first when I went to the military clinic for a yearly checkup shortly after I was married.

"Social Security number, please."

The weary nurse at the family practice clinic front desk shoved a lock of hair out of her eyes and waited not-so-patiently for my answer so she could check me in. I rattled off my own Social Security number. When it didn't match anything in her system, she stifled a laugh, guessing accurately that I'd made the classic rookie mistake.

"No, honey, not *yours*. Your sponsor's."

My sponsor. Steve. Of course. *His* name, *his* Social Security number were now the ticket for me to do anything military-related, to complete the daily tasks of life like buying groceries or accessing medical care. I was a *dependent*. That's the term applied to you once you're married to a military member. And while it's factual, when thrown around carelessly, the word can sound like an insult.

The term *dependent* simply means "someone who's entitled to the benefits, privileges, and rights that come with being the spouse or child of a service member." Many prefer and use the term *military family member* these days, but the official term is still *dependent*. Yet, we are anything but dependent as we forge a life on terms we don't get to choose. We often have to be more independent than our civilian counterparts. We're strong. We're adaptable. Truth be told, we're incredible.

I've come to terms with being called a "dependent" by turning it on its head and making it a positive. Yes, I am dependent on my spouse; and he is dependent on me. That's what marriage is designed for, isn't it? If I ever get to a point where I feel no need for my husband, I think that will be a scary place. We each bring our strengths and weaknesses to our relationship and are truly dependent on each other.

As a long-term military spouse, I've discovered how much my family needs me and how much my husband needs me. I have been the constant in a life full of change. I kept the home fires burning. I was the one who taxied kids to soccer and baseball practice, dance classes, and piano lessons. I researched homeschool support groups, enrichment classes, and co-ops at each new duty station. I was the one who met with teachers, made ER runs, and stayed up at night with scared kiddos while my husband was deployed. I talked my children through middle school drama and budding romances, wiped up vomit. I stretched out my arms in delight as each of our toddlers wobbled toward me, trying out their first timid steps. I was there for the snowball fights, endless PB&Js, sibling squabbles, sticky fingers, and quiet bedtime routines. I was the one who helped unsure teenagers adjust to life in a foreign country, venture into a new friend group, and learn to order food in another language. I coordinated driver's ed classes, standardized testing, and planned college visits back to the States. I was there. For all of it. And what a privilege.

When I was young, I couldn't wait to get away from my hometown and forge my own identity, and that is what I've done as a military spouse. But at heart I'm still that young girl growing up in the warmth of the New Mexico sun. I hope I always keep her wonder. Her ability to pause and take in the moment, to feel the breeze play through her hair, to appreciate good music.

Like the military spouses who've come before me and those who will come after, I've been many things to many people —daughter, niece, granddaughter, student, wife, mother, homeschooler, friend, nurse, writer, pianist, podcaster, and now "Gigi" to my grandchildren. None of these roles completely defines me. I've reinvented myself over and over, sometimes by choice and often by necessity. Military dependent? Yes, in all the helpful, healthy ways of needing my husband, other people, and a supportive community.

All this and so much more. And so are you.

OPPOSITES ATTRACT

When I first met my husband, Steve, in 1986, concerns about the military mission or the impact it would have on my life were admittedly not part of my thoughts. I spent my formative years in a small desert town, part of a family of doctors, teachers, and pastors. My grandparents had settled in the community of Alamogordo in the 1950s and '60s, moving out West from Missouri and Kansas to take jobs and pursue adventure. Alamogordo is near Holloman Air Force Base in Southern New Mexico, so military members and their families were part of the community. I knew these military families came and went every few years, but I still thought of the Air Force as just another job or career choice. I had no concept at all of what being in the military meant beyond what I'd seen in movies and TV shows.

One Sunday evening after church during my senior year of high school, I was chatting and laughing with a friend and a couple of young airmen from the nearby base. I'd played the piano for the worship service and was gathering up my music folder and purse while I bantered with the group. Into the circle strode a handsome young man. He walked straight up to me, stuck out his hand, and said, "Hello, I'm Steve McDonald."

Fumbling with my sheet music, I awkwardly shook hands. Stymied by the suddenness of the introduction, I purposely turned my attention back to the other young men and finished my conversation. Undaunted, Steve stood off to the side and waited patiently to continue talking to me. I was struck by both his good looks and confidence but didn't expect to cross paths with him again.

There were many young adults attending our church, including eligible young women, and besides, I had plans. I intended to move to Oklahoma after graduation to attend a Christian college and pursue my nursing degree.

As the saying goes, "Man plans, and God laughs." The same goes for women, apparently. Steve and I ended up in the same Bible study at church, and I soon learned more about him. We had quite different backgrounds. He'd grown up in humid, woodsy Western Georgia with a retired army father and German mother. I'd always lived in the high desert and mountains of the Southwest, surrounded by extended family. A few years older than me, he had grown up quickly and been on his own since he was seventeen. He enlisted in the Air Force, and Holloman was his first assignment. He was striking, smart, and driven, and though I found myself drawn to him, we often sparred over theological discussions in our Bible study. In fact, I thought he was a bit of a stubborn hothead and he drove me a little crazy. (According to my children, that description could also be applied to me!) But I hadn't yet met anyone who could handle my sass. I was fascinated by his ability to throw my sarcastic one-liners right back at me and match my sometimes dark sense of humor. Sparks were flying, and little did I realize then how much truth there is to the cliché that opposites attract!

One weekend, I had to work and missed an outing with the young adults group to a nearby theme park. I remember thinking, *Well, that settles it—he'll end up dating someone else.* The feeling of losing out surprised me. Later that evening, Steve called to tell me he'd missed me being there and had thought about me all day. My heart leaped as I realized he was interested, too. And that was it! I was hooked, and we began dating. As time went on, I changed my plans of going to school in Oklahoma. I decided to stay in my hometown, take classes at a local college, and continue working. I wanted to see what would happen with this relationship that was unlike any other I had experienced. I look back now and find it amazing that, even though we were so young, we knew this was it. We were married a couple of years later while I was still studying to become a registered nurse.

Now, decades after that first meeting, we are still two stubborn people, bound by love and faith, who can find humor even in the most absurd and difficult times of life. I know God brought us together because He knew exactly what we both needed. Like any couple in a long-term marriage, we've walked through the joyful, mundane, hard, and even tragic times together: miscarriages, deaths of family members and close friends, illness, and way too many natural disasters. (It became a running joke that wherever we'd move would experience the "storm of the century" shortly after our arrival.) It's all woven into the story we've created together. Our stubbornness and grit became the glue that held us together through all the circumstances that came our way. As I write this, we've been married for thirty-five years and have been blessed with four grown children and two precious grandchildren. Even though I had no idea what I was signing up for or how being "married to the military" would change my life, I'm so thankful that Steve interrupted a conversation to make sure we met.

MAKING PEACE WITH MILITARY MARRIAGE

I'd been a military spouse for about a month when I made my first trip alone to the Air Force base where my husband worked. As I walked through the commissary, perusing the produce and canned goods, I clutched my newly acquired military identification, my ID card, in my sweaty palm the entire time. Certain that someone would challenge my right to be there, I kept it close as proof that I did indeed belong.

When I look back on my first commissary shopping venture, my fears about it seem silly. But as a new spouse, I so often worried about looking stupid or ignorant, or about doing things the "wrong way" and reflecting poorly on my husband.

It didn't take long for regular tasks like going to the commissary to become second nature, and I was ready for the bigger demands of military life. Little did I know then what would be required of me, how much the military would affect our marriage and my own life, and how independent I would learn to be. One of the first big hurdles would be saying goodbye to the town and the family I once thought I couldn't wait to leave.

Steve slammed the hatchback on our new-to-us little white Subaru, which was bursting with our luggage and as many belongings as we could cram into it. We turned to face the tearful goodbyes with my parents and my younger siblings who still lived at home.

"You're going to change so much," my mother cried into my shoulder. I refused to believe it, but her words were prophetic.

We clung to each other and wiped tears off each other's faces, stalling to put off the inevitable departure. Steve and I were both in our early twenties and about to set off on our first cross-country move together, far away to his new assignment at Wright-Patterson Air Force Base in Dayton, Ohio.

When we'd learned of our pending move, my cheerful yet naive response had been something like: "Can you tell them this isn't a good time? Maybe they can check back with us later!"

Steve informed me that was not the way the Air Force operated. I would have to accept the inevitable. We then researched and read everything we could get our hands on about what would soon be our new home. To cope with Ohio's cold winters, we convinced ourselves we'd need a four-wheel drive vehicle. Up to that point, we'd both spent our lives in warm climates, and we didn't realize states with cold climates usually kept their roads plowed and treated in snowy weather. Where we both grew up, a light dusting of frozen precipitation could shut down the whole town. So, off we drove in our "car with the knobby wheels" as I called it, me waving back to my family as they grew smaller and smaller in the rearview mirror.

We rolled into Dayton on a cold January day, the sky as gray and unforgiving as my heart. I searched relentlessly for the horizon, which was hidden by the tall trees and hills of Ohio. I'd never lived somewhere without an edge to the landscape like we had in the West. Not being able to see the big sky above me or miles of countryside around me was claustrophobic.

I'd always lived near my family, and soon I was miserable. There's no other word for it. As the weeks went on, a part of my heart told me the cure for my misery was to hold on tightly to the past, to replay memories over and over in my head. Somehow, I thought the answer was to refuse to accept, or even choose to hate, every new thing I experienced. My poor husband.

Everything set me off. A familiar song on the radio, a TV show that was a favorite of my family, the smallest reminder of the past would reduce me to a puddle of inconsolable tears.

My veil of homesickness colored everything, keeping me from seeing what Steve was also experiencing in this new life we were living. It's a bit embarrassing now to remember the level of misery I felt.

Learning that military housing at Wright-Patt would be several months' wait, we quickly found and rented what had been generously termed an "efficiency apartment" in a nearby town. In reality it was one main room plus a tiny kitchenette and an even smaller bathroom. The main room was furnished with a bed and a couch, separated into a "living room" and "bedroom" by a dingy floor-length curtain. The whole place smelled simultaneously dusty and moldy, which is quite a feat. A group of college guys were renting the apartment above us, providing lots of late-night noise and shenanigans.

I spent the next weeks perusing classified ads in the local newspaper for job openings, trying to learn my way around the base, and toting baskets of dirty clothes to the laundromat down the street, where I sat on a cracked plastic chair, penning pages and pages of letters home. Meanwhile, Steve was adjusting to his new job. When I'd return to the miniature apartment, I'd close the faded curtain between our "living space" and "bedroom" and crawl under the covers, which had taken on the stale smell of the rest of the apartment. In the middle of the coldest winter I'd ever experienced, I only wanted to sleep away the homesickness and cold. I was most definitely not interested in blooming where I was planted. I only looked backward, watched the mail for letters from home, ran up long-distance bills calling my mom, and waited for Steve to get off duty. I was certainly not looking for friends or attempting to plug into the community in any meaningful way. We both knew something had to change.

WHO IS THAT GUY?

One evening, I hunched forward in my chair in the church's fellowship hall, figuring if I made myself smaller, no one would notice me or expect me to talk. Still, I couldn't help but over-hear the whispers.

"Who is that man sitting in the foyer?"

"Do you think we should do something?"

"This seems weird."

Finally summoning the courage to speak, I let the other ladies in the women's group know that it wasn't a strange man lurking outside the meeting room in the otherwise empty church—it was my husband.

Steve had driven me to the gathering earlier that evening, reassuring me he'd wait for me right outside until it ended. It was the only way I'd agree to go to an event where I knew no one, and we both knew I needed to make some friends.

Before the move, we'd talked about me taking a break for a few months before I looked for a new nursing job, as my last job before the move had been stressful. It turned out being isolated from everyone besides my husband for weeks on end was not a good thing for either of us. In any marriage, culti-vating other friendships and relationships is important. In a military marriage, it's crucial. For Steve, the pressure of hav-ing to be everyone and everything to me built up and came to a head. One evening he asked me simply and without anger if I would like a one-way plane ticket home, since I seemed so unhappy.

The shock of his question was a wake-up call for me. I stormed out of the room. Well, I stormed from the "living room" side of the room to the "bedroom" side of the room. But slamming the curtain shut didn't offer the sound or satisfaction I hoped for. After my first angry and defensive response, I realized if I wanted our marriage to survive—and I definitely did—something had to change. I was faced with a decision in my life as a military wife: Would I keep wallowing in my misery or move forward?

I made the decision that day to take myself in hand and at least try. I ventured out to several job interviews and ultimately landed a position as a nurse in a downtown teaching hospital. Steve and I found a church and joined a group for young couples. A few months later, we were able to move into military housing and made friends with some of our new neighbors.

Slowly, we forged connections and began to find our way, both individually and together. Choosing to look forward and not constantly back was something I learned to practice each day. I was still homesick, but I was no longer fighting against each step of my new life. I began moving forward willingly, taking small steps toward making a life in our new hometown.

Even as I began to get accustomed to a life far from where I'd grown up, I still didn't comprehend how military life would enfold me over the coming decades.

That twenty-something me was a far cry from the person I am today. I'm so outgoing these days that I often embarrass my children by carrying on conversations with total strangers. I especially reach out to anyone who looks new and unsure at a military event. It's because I still remember that new young military spouse, away from her hometown for the first time, paralyzed at the thought of making small talk, fearful of rejection, unsure how to navigate this big new military world. I'm so thankful she had a sweet young husband who patiently taught her what all the acronyms meant, reassured her she was worth knowing, and pushed her out of her comfort zone when she needed it.

GRATEFUL FOR DEPLOYMENT

Courtney and Dan were newlyweds when he joined the Army not long after 9/11. Courtney agreed with Dan's decision to pursue military service, but like many military spouses, she wasn't prepared for the realities of military life. Dan left for Army basic training when Courtney was thirty-seven weeks pregnant with their first child. Reflecting on that time, Courtney talks about what a shock the situation was.

"I did not feel prepared at all, mostly because we were separated for so long right there in the beginning," said Courtney. "And I felt like I didn't have control in our life. He was off learning how to be a soldier, while I was learning how to be a mom all by myself."

After almost nine months of separation while Dan went through training, they were reunited and stationed at Fort Bliss in El Paso, Texas. Courtney and Dan were acclimating to being new parents and a couple again. At the same time Courtney was navigating the new waters of military spouse life.

"The pressure of being in the Army and learning how to be a military spouse was just a lot of change at once, because I had grown up in a small town my whole life," she said. "I had never had to cope with change, and that was a significant amount of change to deal with at once. I really struggled."

After settling back into life as a family, hoping to enjoy some time together, Dan received orders to deploy for a year. Courtney was stunned.

"To be honest, I didn't cope very well at first. I really struggled with anxiety and depression, but I threw myself into being a mom to my son," Courtney recalled. "I sort of isolated myself. The military was so intimidating and scary to me. Even just going on post. I wasn't aware of the resources available to me, and even if I had been, I'm not sure I would have utilized them. I was just so scared."

The deployment buried an already overwhelmed Courtney under the pressures of balancing life as a new mom with the demands of the military. She knew something had to change.

"I had this lack of control in military life, and that was the root of all my anxiety, not being able to plan. I'm a planner and perfectionist and like to work toward goals, and that can be difficult in military life," said Courtney. "I started to realize that I'm not the one in control anyway. God is. It's one thing to know God is in control, but it's another thing to see it. I struggled, but once I realized what I was struggling with, I learned to advocate for myself. I went and found resources and found the military blogging community. That really helped me so much."

Something else happened, too. Unbeknownst to one another, Courtney and Dan had each embarked on individual faith journeys during the deployment. They'd both struggled with depression during Dan's first year away, and both were searching for guidance and peace. Married life and the military were not what they'd envisioned it would be, and they both realized they would need help.

"It took this really difficult deployment to break each of us down individually on opposite sides of the world to bring us back together with God at the center of our marriage," she said. "While he was deployed, he randomly found a Bible in a stack of giveaway books. And I happened to be walking through Walmart and picked up a Bible one day, too. We were both reading it, and neither of us knew the other was doing it. When we got back together, we realized we had 'his and hers' Bibles—the same edition, same company. It was pretty incredible. I'm so grateful for that deployment now. And I can't believe I'm saying that! But I *am* grateful."

Over the years, Courtney said her marriage has grown stronger than ever, but she hasn't forgotten where they started.

"Family members have said, 'You have such a perfect relationship.' And I've thought, *Is that how it comes across?* It was so hard in the beginning. It's a choice to stay together and work through it. It took us realizing that we can't do it, but God can. We had faith that God could put us back together when we didn't know what to do."

LOVE AND COMPROMISE

Like me, Bryce grew up near a military installation. Though I didn't pay much attention to what military families experienced, Bryce did, and it gave him a bad impression of military life and military marriage.

"I saw the military rip apart families and it was not something that I ever wanted," said Bryce. However, Bryce's outlook has changed. Now a Navy spouse, his experiences have given him a different understanding of military life.

Bryce and his wife, Tracy, had already been married nine years and had three children when Tracy decided to join the Navy. Bryce wasn't thrilled with the idea, based on what he'd seen in his hometown. Fortunately, around that time he connected at church with a retired Air Force couple who became mentors to him and Tracy.

The couple began to look after Bryce and Tracy and initiated a shift in Bryce's mindset regarding military life.

"One thing the husband, Chad, told me was, 'A military family will either come out stronger in the end or it can end up being broken if you allow it to go that way.' And he said, 'Keep your nose to the grindstone during the times that she leaves and do what you have to do. You'll come out stronger, even though it's going to hurt at the time.'"

He describes Tracy entering the military as a "shotgun blast" to his life.

"To be completely honest, I never wanted it," he recalls. Bryce was in a Bible study Chad was leading, and Chad told the group, "Every time we do this particular study, every single time, God pulls someone out of the church to go somewhere."

"I was taking bets on who it was gonna be," Bryce recalled, "not thinking it would be us."

Tracy had initially decided to go into the Air Force but made the decision to join the Navy instead. When she called him from the Navy recruiter's office, Bryce's reaction was humorous.

"I said, 'You can't swim, you don't like large bodies of water, and you're allergic to shellfish.'"

He can laugh about it now, but it was a difficult time for the couple.

"Our marriage almost fell apart and it was due to both of us just having a lot of scars and it came down to our determination," Bryce said. "My mentor said, 'Are you done trying? You need to read 1 Corinthians 13. I want you to start living it because if you want your marriage, you gotta fight for it.' And so that began a four-year process of healing a nearly destroyed marriage. Now we have a very strong marriage. I've been married to this woman for thirteen years, and when she walks into a room, I still get butterflies."

When Tracy became an active-duty sailor, Bryce realized he'd need to form connections and find support for himself and their children. Spouse and family support groups in the military are often female-oriented, which is only natural considering more than 90 percent of military spouses are women.[1] For someone like Bryce, a bearded guy who describes his hobbies as "Bourbon, cigars, and Death Wish Coffee," joining a bunco group or planning luncheons might not have been his chosen pastimes. But he'd decided he was all in with supporting Tracy.

"I told myself, if I'm going to do this, I'm doing it. I'm not one of those guys who will just stand outside of Sephora waiting while my wife goes in," he said. "If I'm not that guy while she's shopping for makeup, then I'm also not going to be that guy while supporting her career. So, I've chosen to be as involved as I can in the Family Readiness Group. I've met some amazing people, and we've got a really good support structure in this command. And if I'm going to be a cheerleader—as horrifying as that image is—I need to be all in and not be that reluctant person in the corner with folded arms, huffing and puffing that I'm here against my will. If I'm doing it, I'm going to be the best I can be."

Bryce's journey from reluctant military spouse to "all in" was not a smooth one, but he is intentional about moving forward. He can relate to other military spouses who bristle at the thought of being labeled a "dependent" or who don't want anything to do with military life. He offers this advice.

"Read through 1 Corinthians 13 in the Bible—and you do not have to be religious to do this. But it's a passage that gets glossed over because it's so often used at weddings. It's like, *Love is patient. Love is kind. Love doesn't remember wrongdoings.* But it's a different perspective when you actually start applying it. What happens when they're not kind? You be kind, you be patient, and you commit to long-suffering. My pastor says that patience is with things and situations; long-suffering is with people because you have to suffer along with them. You take those principles, whether or not you're religious, and you apply them, and you will see a big difference. The goal of any conflict should be to reach reconciliation. And if you've got to compromise, then compromise, because it's better to save the relationship than die on the altar of 'I'm right.'"

Military families certainly aren't exempt from the challenges any couple faces. Those issues come along for the ride in addition to the stresses and changes military life throws at us. We argue and bicker. Sometimes we're too selfish or unnecessarily stubborn like any other couple. Some marriages face bigger problems and are shipwrecked on the rocks of military life and never make it back. We're only human, but there's hope, if we can remember all the reasons we fell in love in the first place. If we try to put each other first, we can make progress toward healing the hurts.

WHEN YOU'RE APART MORE THAN YOU'RE TOGETHER

One summer afternoon, I encountered a handsome man at Reagan National Airport in Washington, DC—a man I hadn't seen in a long time.

One I hoped to see more often.

We exchanged shy glances at the baggage claim, exchanged a few words, a stolen kiss, and then said reluctant goodbyes. Alas, time worked against us and prevented anything further in the interval between my flight arriving and his about to leave, so we enjoyed the few moments granted to us between flights.

True story. The sad part is that the mystery man was my husband—leaving for yet another temporary duty assignment at the same time I was returning home from visiting extended family. We literally did a "Tag, you're it!" handing-off of family responsibilities at the airport terminal. I was delighted to cross paths even for a few minutes, since he'd been traveling for work the entire summer.

When you're faced with a long deployment, advice and encouragement are easy to come by. In fact, people will often come out of the woodwork to commiserate, and to offer help and unsolicited advice. But there's another kind of separation in military life, when your active-duty spouse is home, then gone, then back home, but still mostly gone. He's not really deployed but not really here, either. It's a different military lifestyle vibe, requiring a different balancing act than the long absences of deployment.

During the last decade or so of Steve's military service, many of my friends had never laid eyes on him, much less gotten to know him. He became the stuff of legends in some of my social circles, like the dance mom carpool. I could have given him an exotic name and all sorts of interesting hobbies and weird mannerisms, and no one would have been the wiser. *Xavier couldn't make it today. One of the lions he's training for his circus act needed more rehearsal for the next big show.*

At some point, I became accustomed to offering a lot of explanations and apologies and jokes when arriving at yet another function, kids' event, or even church without my husband, but I stopped doing that. It was tiring, and I figured that the people who needed to know our situation did.

Togetherness—what a wonderful word. When you get married, you're no longer alone. The one you love best has chosen to share their life with you. In a military marriage, it doesn't always feel like that. Most of us don't imagine that our marriage will become a long-distance relationship, but for military spouses, that's the reality we end up with when our spouses are not only away for deployments, but for training or extended duties away from home. It feels like there's no beginning, no end in sight, and you're not sure when "normal" life (whatever that is) will happen again.

Having dealt with this challenge of being apart more than together for many years, I reached a point of reckoning. I realized this is my life and I'd better figure out how to deal with it in some sort of constructive way.

Have I become too independent? When you're alone a lot, you become accustomed to doing everything yourself, eating what and when you want, and making most decisions alone. You also might start to get a little—well, weird. Cereal for dinner or no dinner at all? Makes sense. Reading or watching TikTok till three in the morning? Whatever works. Though I cherished my independence, I also learned how important it was to get back to our normal routines and make my husband feel wanted and needed when he was home.

I've heard that the natural tendency in marriage is to drift apart, and I suppose the divorce rates bear this out. If this is true for partners who are together nearly all the time, how much more so when you're not? Staying connected as a military couple does take some intentionality.

WHERE IS THAT GUY?

"In my defense: I forgot you were home."

It's a little embarrassing to admit, but I spoke those words to my husband when he asked one morning why I hadn't called to say I would be home late the night before. I had been out later than intended with our children at an amusement park. It had slipped my mind to text or call to give him a heads-up about how late we'd be, and I hadn't heard my phone ring when he'd tried to call me. He was gone so much, and I'd become so used to setting my own schedule, I had simply forgotten to update him on my plans. I was relieved when he laughed at my honest answer.

Staying connected mindfully and expressing gratitude are two conscious decisions I learned to make during those years of Steve's frequent absences. We stayed connected through as many avenues as possible, whether by text, video chat, daily calls, or love notes tucked into his luggage. We touched base and shared details of our lives as often as we could.

We also learned—the hard way, of course—how important it was to not take each other for granted. We didn't want to become so focused on our own independent tracks that we lost sight of each other.

One month I took three trips for work and family obligations, not the norm for me. By the last leg of my last flight, I was exhausted from dealing with flight delays, busy airports, and the hassle of travel and crowds. I called my husband to confess, "I couldn't do this on a regular basis like you do. I don't know how you do it."

At that time, while he was constantly in and out of airports, strange hotels, shuttles, and taxis around the world, I usually enjoyed the comfort of my own home and bed. For his part, he often expressed gratitude for all I did to keep things together at home. We realized that it's never productive to play the "who has it harder" game, but infinitely more important to walk a mile in each other's shoes from time to time, and let your partner know how much you appreciate them.

We military spouses do a great job at holding it together. We completely rock at dealing with all the strange circumstances military life throws at us when we're alone. We can manage work responsibilities, relationships, and kid stuff like nobody's business. But I'm married for a reason. I remind myself that I not only love my husband, I also *like* him. I miss the little mundane, day-to-day moments when he's not around, like shopping for groceries together, sitting on the porch watching the sunset, or catching up on our latest reality TV shows. I can make it through the separations. I'm even used to dealing with them, but that doesn't mean they don't affect me.

If you're alone more often than you're not, I'm here to remind you that one day this military life will end and what you put into your relationship now will bear fruit later.

In the meantime, I'd better run. "Xavier" is home and it's time for dinner. Those lions aren't going to feed themselves!

TWO YEARS OF LOVE LETTERS

Many military spouses leave home at a young age when they decide to get married to their service member. Ampy is one example, but when she moved overseas, she was coming to America, not leaving it. A tiny, delicate-boned woman, "Ampy," short for Amperita, filled the room with soft conversation, moving like a small, fluttering bird when I met her at the Bob Hope Village.

With thin, veined hands, she spread out newspaper clippings and faded photos on the table.

"This is Bud," she said. "His real name is Ronald, but everyone called him Bud." Her fingertips traced a photo of a young man in uniform. She spoke of him in both present and past tense as she walked me through their life and her photos.

Ampy was born into an affluent family in Manila, Philippines in the 1930s and was a child when Japanese forces invaded her homeland during World War II. Her family fled into the countryside when Manila was bombed, losing their home and all their belongings except what they'd been able to carry on their backs. Greater losses would follow. Two of Ampy's brothers joined the resistance against the Japanese occupying forces. The family later learned that one brother had been captured, but for months they didn't know either brother's whereabouts. Sadly, they would learn the devastating news that both had been killed. One of Ampy's sisters also died of illness during the war, no doubt due to the hardships and near starvation the family endured. In a final blow, Ampy's mother died, overwhelmed by the pain of losing her children.

"She died of grief," said Ampy. "I remember her always by the window, watching and waiting, with tears down her cheeks."

In our conversation, Ampy meandered through her memories, lingering for a visit with each person and place in her photos. I could tell the years gone by were just as much with her as the warm breeze that filtered through the palm fronds outside her window. I was simply an observer to her reunion with her beloved home country, her loved ones, and especially Bud.

She proudly showed me her beautiful wedding portrait, an oil painting. Bud's airman stripes peek out from the sleeve of his khaki uniform. Tiny white flowers adorn Ampy's shiny black hair. The couple in the painting is serious, and stunning.

"Did you know he wrote me a letter every day for two years?" She pointed to Bud and didn't wait for an answer. "Every day."

Bud was a military police officer in the Air Force, stationed at Clark Field in the Philippines. Ampy worked on the installation as a civilian with Army criminal investigations. The two only crossed paths during shift changes. He manned the night shift, while she took dictation and typed reports during the day. Bud indicated his growing interest by leaving a birthday gift on her desk.

Ampy lived and worked at Clark Field during the week and took the train home to Manila on the weekends. She found herself unable to find a real opportunity to discuss this young American's interest in her with her father.

"My father and I never talked about those things," she said. "We respected our elders, and I didn't even think of going against him. My father did not have a great impression of soldiers. He used to see them take their horses from Fort McKinley to the other camp, and when they'd come back, they'd be drunk, so he was worried about that. My family didn't smoke or drink, and we worked hard. He wasn't against other people; it was just a different lifestyle."

In true keeping with the spirit of romance that triumphs over circumstances, the resourceful, admiring Bud left a romantic note to Ampy every morning on her desk for her to find when she came in to work. Every single morning for two years. Notes turned into shy glances, which morphed into conversations and smiles, and finally into a relationship and a proposal. Letter-writer Bud had managed to overcome any hesitation on Ampy's part.

Racial segregation was common in that era, so Ampy and Bud were inviting controversy with their relationship. Anti-miscegenation laws, prohibitions against interracial marriage, were only beginning to be repealed in the U.S. Still, the path forward had been paved by marriages of American service members to wives from other countries during World War II and the years following. But Ampy was still hesitant to bring up the topic of her American boyfriend to her father.

"It was a different time. We were not allowed to date because of discrimination. I was considered a different race from him."

But as love blossomed, the young couple began to understand that their love for each other meant forever. She finally broke the news of the impending marriage to her father, who seemed accepting but concerned. One of his greatest concerns was whether the marriage would last.

"He said, 'What is going to happen to you?' Because they knew Americans divorce, and there was no divorce allowed in the Philippines at that time."[2]

Another hurdle was being married in her Catholic faith. Unbeknownst to Ampy, Bud was talking to a priest and researching how to convert to Catholicism. He began attending daily Mass with her and was baptized into the church. She asked a prominent local judge she knew to help them with the marriage.

She proudly showed me the marriage certificate signed by him.

"Bud was so mild mannered. I never asked him to convert. He just did it for me," said Ampy. "We were married twice, once by the local justice of the peace and later by the Catholic church."

Though completely in the throes of young love, the newlyweds would meet reality when they moved to the United States. Bud, still on active duty with the Air Force, brought his young wife to meet his family in Oregon.

Bud's mother did not accept the marriage and seemed bent on driving the couple apart. Bud left Ampy with his family for a few weeks while he traveled to Washington state to check into his new assignment and find a place to live. While he was away, Bud's mother was cruel to Ampy. She did not allow Ampy to sleep on the guest bed but told her to sleep on the couch or floor. When Bud returned on weekends, Ampy slept in the bed again, but she didn't say a word to her husband about the arrangement.

"It was just the way things were," she told me. "I really suffered, living with her. She just didn't like me. When Bud was there, she'd open our door in the middle of the night, because you know those old doors don't have keys. So, what we'd do is put a chest of drawers against the door!"

Despite the roadblocks from both society and extended family members, Ampy and Bud were happily married for fifty years until Bud's death. He served for thirty years in the Air Force, including several tours in Southwest Asia during the Vietnam conflict. After his military retirement, they bought a home and settled down in Florida, and they traveled in Europe. Later, Bud embraced a second career as a schoolteacher, and Ampy said he was beloved by his students.

"Honestly, I've had a good life," she said. "We had no problems; really the only problem I ever had was with my mother-in-law. It was such a good life."

Ampy took me on a tour of her travels through her photos: "This one was taken in Switzerland. This one was the Eagle's Nest. This one is Portugal. Here's Paris. I really liked Notre

Dame. We went to Belgium, and you know that was very touching, when you see all the things about our soldiers—it made me cry. And this was taken in the courtyard of the children's school, and this one was the Louvre—"

Her voice trailed off as if she forgot I was there. She moved among her memories with a slight smile curving her lips.

Meeting Ampy was a living reminder that the only things I can control in life are my attitude and my effort. Bitterness is a path we can choose not to follow, like Ampy, who chose to walk the path of joy. During the short time we spent together, Ampy showed me that happiness is truly within us and is ours to embrace, regardless of what others say or do.

LOVE CHANGES EVERYTHING

"He was my one and only," Alice said softly as she showed me a photo of her lifelong love, Stan. Young and smiling, Alice and Stan look like movie stars in the black and white photos.

Over the course of an afternoon at the Bob Hope Village, Alice shared newspaper clippings, vintage photos, and loving words about her beloved Stan, who died in 2000, when the couple had been together nearly fifty years. Looking at the family portraits of Alice, Stan, and their grown children, it was easy to see that the movie star looks run in the family.

"That's me when I joined the Air Force back in 1951," she said. In the photo she indicates a young woman with glossy dark hair and a bright smile leaning casually against a car, with one hand shading her face from the sun. I could see hope splashed across her face—the expression of a girl who could see life holding endless possibilities.

The face in that photo is a long way from her earlier years. Alice grew up in the 1930s and '40s in a family that would have been considered below the poverty level. She said her father was an alcoholic, known around town for all the wrong things, and her mother worked to support the family. Alice was left to tend to her younger sister. Still, she didn't recall feeling unhappy.

"Back in those days, we just didn't know any better," she said.

During her high school years, Alice was inspired by a teacher who shared tales with her class about her time serving in the Army during World War II and later living in England. Alice came to realize this was a life she wanted, too.

"I loved writing, reading, music," she said. "When my teacher asked me what I wanted to do with my life, I was stumped. I simply had no idea. I couldn't think beyond what my life was. After all, I was just the daughter of the town drunk."

Inspired by her teacher, Alice began the process of joining the Air Force. Once she passed the physical screening
and other requirements, she found herself on a troop train
with other recruits headed for basic military training. "Basic"
is not something most military members remember fondly.
They usually tell stories of harsh training instructors, taste-
less chow hall food, constant tests of physical endurance and
mental toughness, and endless marching in formation. But
not Alice. She thrived on the structure and seeming abundance, including indoor plumbing.

"I loved basic training!" she said with a grin. "My friends
teased me about how many showers I took, since I suddenly
had access to hot running water. We had regular food, clean
sheets—everything I'd always dreamed of. Luxury!"

Alice said her father was a belligerent, racist man, and
she'd been taught to avoid people who weren't like her family.
For her, the multicultural nature of military life held a great
fascination, and she embraced the idea of making friends
from other backgrounds.

The Air Force sent her to Keflavik, Iceland, where she
was assigned to a unit with five thousand men. If you think
a young, naive girl from a small town was intimidated, think
again. Alice said being one of only a handful of female airmen
was "wonderful!"

"Growing up, I never felt good enough. Boys wouldn't date
me because of my clothes or my father, and suddenly I felt
besieged."

Surprisingly, though, she didn't go on many dates.

"I was picky!" she said. "I didn't want a man who drank
because I'd had enough of that growing up."

The enlisted club, a Quonset hut on the base in Iceland,
was a natural gathering place for the military members stationed at the remote location. One evening, a handsome,

curly-headed man approached Alice and asked her out on a date. She promptly turned him down and he asked why.

"Because you've been drinking," Alice told him frankly. She didn't want her bright future to be dimmed by anything like the alcoholism she'd seen in her father.

The next night, the persistent young man reappeared.

"I haven't had a drop to drink," he said and asked her to dance.

Here she paused mid-story, remembering. Listening to her, I could feel the memories lifting her from the room and far away.

"And that was it," she said, breaking the silence. "I'd found the love of my life."

Around the time Alice and Stan met, the Air Force held a worldwide singing competition for a new entertainment ensemble called Tops In Blue. Alice was selected as the first woman to perform with the group. [3]

After Alice finished her stint with Tops In Blue, she and Stan were sent to different duty stations, she to Maryland and he to Ohio. When their request to be transferred to the same base was denied by the Air Force, Alice understood that it wasn't possible to be with Stan and continue serving in the military. Keeping active-duty couples together—even if they were married—was not a military priority in the 1950s, so Alice made the tough decision to leave active duty. She was honorably discharged from the Air Force in 1954 and married Stan a few months later at Wright-Patterson AFB.

Over the next decades, Stan enjoyed a successful Air Force career, retiring as a chief master sergeant. Alice pursued a career in the civil service, volunteered, and raised their children. The family moved around the world, as military families do, creating a home in locations as varied as Little Rock, Arkansas and Misawa, Japan. They made it through Stan's tours in Korea and Vietnam. When Stan retired and came home for good, they reveled in their time together, traveling and playing golf. They laughed a lot. And yes, they kept dancing.

"I know God sent me to Iceland to meet him. I loved him so much."

After Stan died, Alice struggled with what she should do next, what her life would look like without her Stan.

"We had a beautiful Florida room," she recalled about the sad days after his death. "One day, I was sitting in Stan's chair and facing the windows. This gray mist came through the room where I was sitting in a chair, crying. The mist stopped in front of me, and I felt my husband telling me to go to the Bob Hope Village. People will think I'm crazy, but I felt it so strongly and so I called them right away."

She sold her home in just over a month, packed up her belongings, and moved into the Bob Hope retirement community. She didn't want to sit wishing away the years or racked with regret over things undone. Instead, she continued to travel and try new adventures, like zip-lining and bungee jumping.

She said she wanted to treasure and remember her beloved Stan, while still creating a new chapter of her own, by involving herself with a circle of friends, volunteering, and planning events like the yearly Bob Hope Memorial Charity Golf Classic. And she still sings—sometimes.

After some prompting from me and demurs from her that "My voice will crack," Alice agreed to sing part of "Night and Day," a favorite Frank Sinatra standard she once loved to perform.

"... *let me spend my life makin' love to you . . . Day and night, night and day . . .* "

The last note hovered in the air, ringing with longing, love, and loss.

I recorded my conversation with Alice, and when I got back home and listened again to the song, I could hear myself in the background sniffling, searching in my purse for a tissue. Hearing the song again, this time with the stillness and distance between me and Alice, I wiped away the tears. I felt every note and every word all over again.

One of the last things she said to me during our afternoon together was, "My life has been absolutely unbelievable."

I walked away from my time with her, changed. I learned so much from her. Lessons that are not new, but as fresh for military spouses today as they were for Alice:

Recognize love when you see it and don't wait.

Happiness is within your grasp. Go get it.

Life is short and goes by more quickly than we'd like to think.

Don't wait to tell the ones you love how much they mean to you.

And the biggest lesson of all:

Don't be bound by your past, what other people say you are, or even what you once were. Life is truly amazing and yours for the taking. And love has the power to change everything.

FINDING THE WORDS

Dolores grew up on a sugar cane plantation on Kauai, one of the islands of Hawaii. She was ten years old when the Japanese attacked Pearl Harbor and threw the U.S. into World War II. Soon, American troops began arriving in large numbers to fortify the Hawaiian Islands, and what had been a quiet happy life surrounded by local aunties and schoolmates changed forever.

"We had to carry around gas masks, keep our ID cards on us at all times, and everything was rationed. We sure grew up in a hurry," Dolores recalled.

After the war, Dolores's aunt married an American military man and moved to Savannah, Georgia. On a visit to see her aunt, Dolores met James, her future husband. Though in love and excited to make a new life with James, Dolores was heartbroken to leave her island home behind. She would face more difficulties while adjusting to American culture and life as a military wife. She encountered racism, even from some of her new husband's family members. However, Dolores said her mother-in-law was completely supportive from the beginning.

"She'd light up like a light bulb when I walked into a room," said Dolores. "I could see that she loved me."

Accustomed to using Hawaiian pidgin in her everyday speech (a combination of English, Hawaiian, and other immigrant languages) Dolores found speaking only English to be a struggle.

"I wanted to speak well, but no matter what I did, I had an accent. I practiced so hard, trying to speak correctly, that my jaws actually hurt. I finally decided, 'I am who I am.' There was a lot of prejudice in the fifties and sixties. It did bother me sometimes, but it was nothing compared to what the wives who came over from Germany went through."[4]

These days, when she encounters someone with a preconceived notion about her, she doesn't take it to heart.

"I've outgrown that. I know who I am, and I'm a good person. If you turn your nose up at me, I feel sorry for you that you don't know me and you're missing out. Before, I wanted to please everybody. Not anymore."

James served in the Navy during World War II, then later transferred to the Air Force where he served for another twenty-six years. He and Dolores had two sons, Steven and Paul. They moved every few years during their time in the Air Force, and she missed her family back in Hawaii desperately.

"That first Christmas," she remembered, "I tried to call them but couldn't get a call through because the lines were busy. So, I tried again on New Year's, and when my mother answered, all I said was, 'Mama,' and then I broke down. We hardly spoke. We just listened to each other cry."

Military life took Dolores and James and their family all over the world, including to bases in Germany, California, Okinawa, Wisconsin, and Michigan, and to their last assignment in Florida.

"Every time you move you have to give up everything. But once we got settled in a house, I just made a home for us," she said. "Every base was my favorite! I've always looked for the positive, and I love the military family. Military people are the best people in the whole world."

Her outlook on life helped Dolores thrive. Rather than wishing for what had been, Dolores made a point of creating a happy life wherever she landed. After James retired from the Air Force, the couple bought a home in Satellite Beach, Florida and settled into enjoying more time together. Dolores worked as a cashier and baker at the local high school and loved connecting with students. She and James traveled, often with friends, and went fishing together. When James found out he had lung cancer, the doctors gave him six months to live. Instead, he lived for another sixteen months. Dolores quit her job to stay home and care for him.

"I was so concerned that he'd be okay when he died, and I'd worry about what would happen to him when he was gone. He told me, 'When I die, I'll come back as a butterfly so that you know I'm all right.'"

One morning, their priest called to see if they needed anything, and Dolores asked if he'd come by to anoint James and pray for him. After the priest's visit, she and a close friend sat near James's bed, chatting about their past adventures together. James joined in the conversation, adding his own memories. It was peaceful and calm. After a while, he softly said, "When you travel, think of me."

Dolores and the friend agreed that of course they would. After a few minutes, Dolores realized James had gone completely still.

"And just like that, he was gone," she said. "It was so peaceful. I didn't know those would be his last words to me. I didn't know the priest would be giving him his last rites that day. But I'm so glad he went that way."

In one quiet moment, it was over. Forty years of marriage, love, togetherness, shared hardship, raising children, all ended without fanfare. Struggling to accept the fact that her James had left this earth, Dolores wandered out to her back yard, attempting to gather up the shards of her broken heart before facing the practical matters to come.

She stepped outside and found the yard full of butterflies. She remembered what James said about coming back as a butterfly.

Tears slid down her cheeks as she watched the butterflies hovering and dancing among the flowers and trees. To her, it was a sign from God that James was all right and she wasn't alone.

Fifteen years later, Dolores left her home in Satellite Beach and moved into an apartment at the Bob Hope Village where she could continue to live independently. She's continued to travel, including visits to Singapore and her beloved Kauai, along with accepting some speaking engagements.

"The Air Force asked me to come to Washington to speak and it ended up being fun. I spoke to about a hundred and fifty top military people. A civilian contractor came up to me and said, 'You look like a friendly face.' We ended up talking while we waited. I saw all the generals and chiefs coming in, and I told that lady I was nervous. She said, 'You'll be fine, talk to them like you're talking to me!' And I looked around the room and thought, *My children are older than these people! I can do this!*"

And the woman who'd once been embarrassed by her accented English did just that—gave an amazing, well received speech. She found the words to express the beauty of the love and the life she had chosen for herself.

PART 2

ADVENTURE STORIES

CELEBRATING THE UNEXPECTED

Traveling—it leaves you speechless, then turns you into a story-teller. —Ibn Battuta

Pulling off the DC Beltway into the nearest gas station, I stuck my credit card into the gas pump's card reader and the nozzle into my car's tank. The pump beeped and gave me one simple instruction: "Enter zip code."

My mind went completely blank.

What is my zip code? Okay, seriously. What is it?

The pump continued its insistent beeping.

Am I experiencing a stroke? Early-onset dementia? What on earth is my zip code?

I frantically searched the recesses of my tired brain but came up empty—like my gas tank. Giving up on my brain, I began rummaging through my purse and found the scrap of paper where I'd scrawled our latest address. We had just moved—for the sixth time in as many years—and the zip code hadn't yet taken root in my mind. Wonder why?

I've since heard from other military spouses who experienced the same forgetfulness of zip codes, phone numbers, and even places. Do you ever get in your car to drive to a nearby Target, and realize the directions your brain is giving you from "home" to "Target" are from two duty stations ago? Or is that just me?

The "certainty of uncertainty" has become something of a mantra in the military spouse world, a truth you learn to embrace. The only thing you can count on is that your reality will keep changing. Your spouse has orders to a new duty station? Hold on because that could change at a moment's notice. Feeling settled after a couple of years at a new location? Well, brace yourself, because a move is right around the corner. Have vacation plans set in stone? (Yes, it's okay if you just laughed out loud.) Temporary duty or deployment orders have a way of showing up the moment you click the final "purchase" button on an all-inclusive vacation package or airline tickets. That's why you always buy the travel insurance and always use a pencil when marking your calendar.

How do military spouses start over again and again and again? I'm not sure I know the answer, even though I repeated this cycle for more than thirty years. We learn to expect the unexpected and even to celebrate it.

Say hello. Jump in. Get the feeling of being settled. Keep in mind this is in no way permanent. Get orders. Move on.

Simply put, it's a crazy way to live—the repeated uprooting and replanting that so many military families experience. Why would anyone choose this? Perhaps military spouses are gifted with a sense of adventure. Whether it's innate or tends to grow as each new chapter unfolds is anybody's guess.

Though I couldn't always remember my zip code, I did learn to embrace the flurry of moving and the challenge of resettling. From the snowy mountains of Germany to the verdant mountains of Oahu, I began to realize how very blessed I was to experience the adventure of military life and all the places it sends us.

HOME IS WHERE THE AIR FORCE SENDS US

One of the strangest things about long-term military service is what it can do to your sense of time. My memories are housed in my mind—in compartments labeled with the place we were stationed when they occurred, with a subheading of other significant events, like which number deployment we were going through. Steve asked me the other day about a family memory from 2007. I shuffled through the compartments in my brain and thought back.

"We were in North Dakota at the time, weren't we? Wait, no—2007—we were at Beale by then since we were stationed there from '06 to '08."

I've also won many an argument with family members over what happened when. I'm the keeper of our family's varied who-what-when-where-how milestones: where babies were born, which places we lived apart from my husband for the majority of a duty station, when a particular child had an ER visit.

"No, it couldn't have happened then! We were in California at that point, not Florida," I'll chirp in response to a question about when a certain child sprained an ankle.

Maybe it's an odd skill to be proud of, but everyone needs a superpower. Mine is keeping all the duty stations and family events straight. With a family of six people and about three times as many moves, it's no small feat.

We once had a wall hanging we displayed in our many homes over the years. We'd bought it at a base arts and crafts fair, a wooden plaque showing a cheerful message hand-painted in cursive, "Home Is Where the Air Force Sends Us." Very shabby chic, which was popular at the time. It came with a set of smaller blank plaques, where we could write our new assignment each time we moved. These hung from stylish metal hooks, in order, displaying our journey though military life. Though beautiful and meaningful, we ended up stowing the wall hanging in a closet a few years later, because the Air Force had sent us to so many locations that we ran out of plaques.

This globe-trotting doesn't seem abnormal in military circles. It's only when you talk to someone who's still living in the same neighborhood, town, or even home they did when they first married twenty or thirty years ago that you remember: This isn't normal. Neither are some of the things we do when moving, like making creative dinners with the last remnants of the pantry. Ramen and mustard surprise, anyone?

We know it won't last forever, but experienced military spouses know the upheaval of transition can go on for weeks or even months. Moving overseas or taking concurrent leave adds to the wait time, and often we end up waiting or looking for housing longer than expected when we roll into a new location.

By the time he retired, Steve had fifteen military assignments and we'd lived in eighteen different houses. With the misplaced optimism of an armadillo crossing the road, with each move I was convinced that *this* would be the one I conquered—instead of it conquering me. Each time I made checklists for my checklists, created spreadsheets, tried move-organizing apps, and pumped myself up believing *this* would be the move I'd absolutely kill it and wow everyone with my organizing expertise.

"How *does* she do it?" the neighbors would wonder in amazement.

"Look at her, so unruffled, so put together, yet—so organized!" my family would crow.

In my imaginary scenario, everything would go exactly as planned, and even if it didn't, unflappable me would handle it.

And then came reality.

The moving company would have a scheduling glitch at the last minute and our moving and packing dates would all change; or the whole family would be hit with a violent twenty-four-hour bug right before our carefully-planned-to-every-last detail-except-for-the-possibility-of-flu move. Oh, and of course, that was also the time we decided to do a DITY—or do-it-yourself—move. Now the military calls it a "personally procured move," or "PPM," but whatever you call it, it's hard to do it all yourself when all your individual selves are sick.

Planning and preparing are very much part of my personality. Planning ahead helps me feel ready for a transition, but let's face it, there's no way to foresee the unforeseeable. Believe me, moving a family of six around the world is a lesson in what can go wrong and how many things can go wrong.

MOVING TALES

Once upon a time, a family was moving overseas and discovered their passports missing—after their whole house had been packed. Yes, that was us. And yes, we had set aside a "do not pack" area with signs which the movers had cheerfully ignored. As I recall, *someone* panicked, shrieking something along the lines of, "Oh my gosh, we will never be able to board our flights!" and running around the house searching every drawer, cupboard, and suitcase. And by *someone*, I mean me. Fortunately, we were able to gain access to the warehouse where our boxes had been deposited before being shipped. It must have been our lucky day, because Steve found all six passports after rummaging through a few boxes. The crisis was averted, and *someone* was able to calm down.

Strange things can happen when your whole life is regularly boxed up by strangers. I once unpacked a box that had been in government storage for six months and discovered an open bottle of Tabasco sauce at the bottom, along with a half-eaten, moldy, green sandwich. But no one in our family uses Tabasco. Another time I found a Snickers bar with only one bite out of it. I knew for certain none of our four voracious teens would abandon a candy bar after just one bite. In a more destructive misadventure, packers had chunked my husband's thirty-five- and fifty-pound weights in the bottom of our antique German china cabinet. The packers on the receiving end, who'd had nothing to do with the travesty, pitied me as I mourned over the cracked cabinet. One patted my shoulder awkwardly as I cried.

Moving with pets adds an extra layer of stress to a move, especially an overseas one. First, there's the paperwork and hoops you must jump through to get your pet in and out of different countries and even states; then, there's the travel itself. When we were moving back from Germany, our first flight was delayed, making us late for the next one. When we landed, we ran to catch our next flight and saw the gate close just as we ran up. Unable to book another flight until the next day, Steve wrangled with making hotel arrangements for our family, while I tried to determine where our dog, Toby, was. Had he already been loaded onto the flight we'd just missed? Was he sitting in a storage facility somewhere? No one could seem to tell us anything. My two middle schoolers were both in tears at this point, and I nearly was, too. Finally, we decided to walk down to lost baggage to see if we could find some help. Approaching the baggage desk, I heard a faint whine behind me and the unmistakable sound of Toby's tail thumping against his crate. We'd walked right past him, but he must have recognized his family. All of us breathed a sigh of relief.

One late-year move found us eating Christmas dinner after having hurriedly shoved our unpacked boxes into any available space. We had moved in October, an overseas-to-overseas move on short notice orders, so our household goods had taken quite a while to arrive. We finally received our shipment a few days before Christmas, so we unpacked as much as we could to make the place livable: furniture, kitchen, beds, and bedding. Then we crammed the rest into the garage to deal with later so we could enjoy our Christmas celebration. And we did! We put together a hurried dinner and invited new neighbors over for commissary-bought pie. All were military families, so no explanations were needed for the lack of décor and not-from-scratch dessert. It was one of the simplest, most joy-filled holidays in memory.

The transitions, goodbyes, and crazy things that happen during a move don't necessarily get easier the more you move, but your coping skills and strength will grow. Believe it or not, when you finally make the transition into retirement and civilian life, you might just miss the excitement and even the stress of moving just a teensy bit.

I don't—yet. But you might.

THINGS THAT MAKE YOU GO, "HOOAH!"

I shuffled across the bedroom on a middle-of-the-night bathroom quest, trying to maintain the half-awake state that would allow me to fall quickly back to sleep when I returned to my warm bed. Unfortunately, in the darkness my big toe made painful contact with the steel toe of a combat boot. Grabbing my throbbing foot, I hopped in pain, suppressing the urge to cry out and wake my sleeping husband. It would have served him right if I did, because his boot was the culprit.

Dad-blammit! It's like an obstacle course in here. Why can't he put his boots away?

Mission complete, I snuggled under the covers, wide awake, thanks to my throbbing toe. Lying in the dark, I remembered waking in the dead of the night just a few weeks before and being unsettled by the silence of the room, sleeping alone again. Steve was in the midst of a gone-more-than-home phase of his Air Force career, and his wayward boot couldn't make me too annoyed, because it meant he was with us. At least for a few days.

His home-again, gone-again schedule was fraught with confusion and strange happenings. One night, when Steve was away for a few days, I was awakened by a gentle snore near my ear. This was not the sound of one of my children who had climbed into bed with me—as they sometimes did when he was gone. This was a full-grown-human noise. I held my breath, paralyzed with fear, mind racing.

Who is in bed with me?

I kept a small butterfly knife in the drawer of my nightstand for just such an occurrence. (Yes, I am equal parts nutty *and* prepared.) So, I began to reach for it slowly, plotting my next move. Hand on the drawer knob, I froze, as the person next to me shifted around and emitted an alarming, yet strangely familiar sound.

"Harrrummph—Gurgle—Blerg—Snore—"

Oh, yeah. I'd forgotten Steve had been due home late the night before. He must have arrived after I'd fallen asleep and slipped into bed without waking me. *Yikes.* I drew my hand back from the bedside table and its dangerous contents. Lucky for both of us, I'm a slow mover when I first wake up.

It's curious the things you get used to in military life, whether it's routinely tripping over combat boots or waking up with a "stranger" in your bed. Some realities become such an ingrained part of your life that you don't realize how odd it all is until someone outside the military bubble mentions it or your service member leaves the military.

Let's face it, there are some strange, difficult, and sometimes stupid things you get used to in military life.

Forgetting your own Social Security number: It's ingrained in me that my "sponsor's Social" is my admission ticket for everything in military life. When someone asks for my Social Security number, I still have to think twice, while my husband's rolls off my tongue with the speed and ease of a longtime auctioneer.

Long-distance marriage: When I first got married, I didn't realize I'd be spending so much time apart from my husband. When Steve was deployed or away on temporary duty (TDY), I was ever so grateful for the ability to video chat when that option was available. Past generations would have marveled at our technology, but the delays, dropped calls, and frozen screens are still poor substitutes for being together. Sleeping alone night after night and the prolonged lack of intimacy wears on you, too. Not to mention all the decisions you'll make alone, both big and small, and special moments and milestones missed. I certainly wasn't expecting to go through labor and deliver a big-headed baby without my husband there to blame—I mean—help. I don't recommend this scenario if you can avoid it.

The separations and goodbyes don't get any easier; you just get stronger. You learn from each experience, adding coping tools to your toolbelt.

Making a will when you're young: Before a deployment, military couples—even young ones—know they need to create wills, powers of attorney, and other legal documents. This may sound morbid to some, but there's nothing wrong with preparing for what life may throw your way. Even in civilian life, more young people should probably consider and prepare for these eventualities, but why would they when the need seems so distant? In military life we are often brought close to the fragility and uncertainty of life. We know to be prepared with the right documents and to appreciate every precious moment.

You talk funny: The military certainly loves its acronyms. Perhaps you've already heard of TDY or TAD, BAH, COLA, and PCS (which stands for "permanent change of station," even though we know it's not permanent). These are only the beginning. My advice to new spouses is to make a cheat sheet right now, whether you're attempting to remember the symbols for your spouse's unit or decipher important strings of letters like DEERS, CONUS, OCONUS, or AAFES.

The acronyms and other military lingo will become part of your vocabulary, and you'll find yourself uttering words strange enough to make civilians raise an eyebrow or two. "What's your sitrep? Yeah, I got your six. Foam the runway, he's comin' in hot! Semper Gumby! Get comfortable being uncomfortable, because the only easy day was yesterday."

(Check the glossary at the end of this book for these and other military terms and acronyms.)

Afterburners and other background noises: As a military spouse you get used to having armed guards at the entrance of your neighborhood and security forces strolling around the food court at the Exchange, the military's version of a department store. Stopping to let a military convoy pass by becomes part of a normal day—you just scroll your phone while you wait, unimpressed. Driving past a runway full of fighter jets that look straight off the set of *Top Gun* won't even make you blink. You hear so much aircraft noise and/or artillery fire that you don't hear it at all. It's just the background noise of your everyday life. At least that's been true for me.

Some sounds, however, I never get tired of and rarely ignore, even after many years. Reveille, "The Star-Spangled Banner," and "Taps" are all played daily on military installations. These songs sound like home to me now. The sad notes of "Taps" carrying over the waning evening light is sobering. I still get teary eyed whenever I hear it, and I hope that never changes.

Embracing your plan B or C or D: Military life is constantly changing. Military spouses learn not to get too wedded to PCS orders, a location, or even a home. I've completely unpacked in military housing only to have the housing office direct us to move to another house on base just months later.

When we were in Germany, Steve got orders for our next move while he was on a long deployment. All the preparation for our move back to the States would have to be done before he returned. On my own, I made arrangements to ship our vehicle, dealt with the mountain of paperwork, and handled the move with our four kids. After several days with packers and movers, I stood in the doorway of our home, exhausted. I watched the last moving truck trundle down the street with our household goods loaded and marked for shipment to Arizona. In a scenario I could not have made up—even if I'd wanted to, and I didn't—the phone rang at the exact moment the last truck turned the corner. It was my husband, calling to tell me our orders had been changed to Hawaii. For a split second, I considered running after the trucks to try and stop them. Not that it would have helped, but it seemed reasonable for a moment. I couldn't believe I would need to redo all the paperwork, and reroute the family car, which I'd already shipped. Somehow it all worked out; the military does take care of its own. And though I hear Arizona is nice, I really can't complain too much, since we did get to move to Hawaii.

Sometimes plan B turns out to be the best plan after all.

Saying goodbye when you're not leaving: In military housing or in a military-heavy neighborhood, the typical PCS season from May to September brings a multitude of moving vans, empty houses, and goodbyes. Even if you're not moving, your calendar will be full of hail and farewell gatherings, changes of command, and retirement ceremonies. Even when you're not moving, you and your children will often have to say goodbye to friends who are. Moving is hard, but being the ones left behind can be even harder. Give yourself grace for these hard seasons and be aware of how your children are taking it.

All. The. Curtains: After a number of moves, you may end up with a collection of window coverings to rival IKEA. The flip side of that is that you'll also get to live with a wide range of window styles in a large number of homes: modern, ranch, historic, or stairwell apartments. All this experience will help you figure out what is essential for your "forever home." I know it helped me.

Murphy's Law: You've heard of Murphy's Law: Anything that can go wrong, will go wrong. Perhaps it comes as no surprise that this truism has military origins.[1] And for very good reasons, military spouses have created their own corollary to Murphy: Anything that can go wrong will go wrong—*as soon as your spouse leaves on deployment.* Something will always break or go kaput. Every time my husband left home, I hoped that *this time* my best laid plans would foil Murphy's nefarious ones. Every time I was wrong. Finally, I learned to expect Murphy, embrace it, and even find humor in the absurdness. Murphy's Law is a great contributor to every military spouse's strong sense of humor. The fact that we are able to manage so much on our own—everything up to and including childbirth, if necessary—proves what we already know: Military wives are tough as nails.

In spite of the oddities of military life, somehow we always find a way to embrace hope and create a life right where we are. Now that my husband is retired, I won't say I miss tripping over steel-toed combat boots in the middle of the night. But I admit to having a certain nostalgia for the thrill I used to feel at the sight of his boots by the door, reminding me: He's home!

MOVING WITH CHILDREN

When we moved from Texas to Florida, we did a partial DITY ("Do-it-yourself") move, meaning we transported some of our belongings ourselves. Our four children were aged eight and under, and our baby, Anna, was not the kind of baby who was lulled to sleep by riding in the car. In fact, she hated being in her car seat. She would strain in protest as soon as she felt the car seat straps touch her little shoulders. It set her off that anyone had the audacity to restrain her in the car. So, naturally, we thought it only made sense to spend several days on the road, caravanning across the Southern U.S. with me driving the minivan, Steve in his truck, each vehicle pulling a rented trailer, with four kids divided between us.

Those days were a blur of crying and potty stops. Steve's mom, Friede, God bless her, offered to come along with us on the trip as an extra pair of hands. As long as she was strapped into her car seat, Anna cried. Friede, "Oma" to our kids, was distressed by hearing the baby sound so inconsolable. I was too, but I also knew it wouldn't matter what we did; Anna was simply going to cry until she fell asleep. She only wanted to be held, but we had to get in the car and drive at some point and actually get there and put an end to our misery. So onward we pressed while Oma patted Anna's tummy until she succumbed to her tiredness and fell asleep. After that, we didn't dare stop for fear Anna would wake up and start the whole scene over again. Have to potty? Better hold it. Need a drink? Rummage around and find a forgotten half-bottle of something on the floorboard and hope for the best. When we rolled into MacDill Air Force Base in Tampa, Florida, I swore we'd never, never do that again. But of course, we did. Selective PCS amnesia is real.

Kids certainly have a way of making a move interesting. As parents, we're worried about the logistics of transition, finding new schools, and looking for ways for them to connect with potential friends, sports, and activities. But it's the unknowns of transitions with kids that kept us on our toes.

Years after The Mighty Crying Road Trip, we moved from Hawaii to a new assignment in Virginia. Our oldest son was married, and the other had opted to stay behind in Hawaii to finish college. It was strange to move with only Steve, me, and our younger two girls who were both now teenagers. One of the girls had a particularly difficult time adjusting and let us know in no uncertain terms.

"Why did I have to move?"

"I wish I could have stayed with my friends!"

"Why did you do this to me?"

I felt so helpless as a parent, watching her struggle and feeling there was little I could do to help her get through the process. Her feelings mirrored my own in so many ways. We spent a hot sticky summer in temporary lodging waiting for a house, and none of us were very excited about the transition.

Over the years, each of our four children struggled with moving at one time or another. It can be hard to know what to do for the ones you love the most. Each child is different from every other, and the same transition that shakes one's entire world is merely a blip for another. Our kids seemed to take turns with difficulties adjusting. As they got older with more moves under their belts, the excitement of a new location was often dampened by leaving friends and having to be the new kid yet again.

We did our best to put into practice all the moving advice intended to help military kids adjust—host goodbye parties for their friends, walk through all the healthy ways to say farewells, explore the new location, help them make new connections. No matter what you do, it's not uncommon for military kids to struggle mightily after a big move. Ours did.

I empathized with my children, realizing it can be overwhelming to have your whole world upended in childhood. When they were little, I knew we were leaving the only home they might remember at that point in their lives. As they grew, they had to leave the places where they'd made their very best friends.

Being a parent of military kids requires a bit of blind faith in trusting that things will get better at some point, and patience to let children get there on their own timetable. Don't hesitate to seek outside help when needed. Children don't process transitions on their parent's schedule—or anyone else's. As parents, we need to accept that, listen to their concerns, and let them express their fear and grief. There's no magical formula to make it all better, but you can walk through it with them. Leaning into the discomfort and letting them express what they need from us can be uncomfortable and even scary, but it's necessary. Their sadness is not something we can fix, but we can be there for them and with them.

JOINING THE OVERSEAS CLUB

For Steve's first fifteen years on active duty, we watched enviously as other military friends moved overseas and back again. We listened patiently as they reminisced about sipping hot mugs of *Glühwein* at German Christmas markets or learning to scuba dive off the beautiful shores of Okinawa. We wanted to be part of that club and have our own stories to tell.

Then, Steve got orders to Andersen Air Base on the island of Guam. Finally! We were invited to the overseas club, and we were ready for initiation. The day our family left for Guam, we showed up at the airport with four kids and eighteen pieces of luggage. Yes, eighteen. Don't judge. We made use of the maximum allowed, knowing our household goods would take several months to arrive at our new home on the other side of the world. Though Guam is a U.S. territory, it's closer to Japan than it is to any U.S. state, including Hawaii. Getting to this remote island in the western Pacific required many hours of travel for our family, beginning with the coast-to-coast trip from Florida to California. From there we flew five-plus hours to Hawaii, and from there took an eight-hour-long flight to Guam. With layovers, by the time we arrived we'd been traveling for nearly twenty-four hours straight.

Our flight arrived on Guam after dark. Descending the stairs that led from the aircraft's interior down to the runway, we were instantly engulfed by overpowering humidity. Friends warned me about the heat and humidity on the tropical island, but I scoffed, reminding them that we'd just spent several years in Florida. How much worse could it be?

A lot, apparently. We slogged alongside other passengers exiting the aircraft, helping our four young children maneuver themselves and their laden backpacks safely down the narrow stairs to the tarmac. Hearing our eleven-year-old son's cry for help, I turned back and saw his glasses had completely fogged over. He was struggling under the weight of his heavy backpack and trying to see where he was going, while holding his little sister's hand. I rushed to help him. Poor guy. Yes, this was a different humidity entirely.

After crossing more miles and time zones than we cared to count, we had arrived. We were promptly rescued by our sponsor, whom we came to call Sergeant Nick. He rolled up to the Guam International Airport in a battered minivan, an unlit cigarette dangling from one corner of his mouth, and cheerfully loaded up our family of six and our pile of luggage. If he was surprised or alarmed by the sight of our exhausted, disheveled family and our numerous suitcases, he didn't show it. One of our children had a cast on his arm after a last-minute visit to the ER the night before boarding our overseas flight. Another had been repeatedly airsick on the long journey, and all of us were a little heartsick about the friends and family we had left behind. It's no stretch to say we were not at our best in that moment. Sergeant Nick took it all in stride, and he made all the difference in the world to us during our first days in a new place and culture. Having a good sponsor gets any overseas assignment off to a good start.

Each branch of the military administers an overseas sponsorship program, in which military families moving overseas are assigned a sponsor. A sponsor is an active-duty person—usually someone from your spouse's unit—who serves as a point of contact before the move, welcomes the family on arrival, and helps with transition throughout. Often, the sponsor helps with practical matters like temporary lodging, transportation from the airport, and information about military housing. A sponsor can also provide important details ahead of time, such as local school options and requirements for bringing pets to overseas locations.

Sergeant Nick didn't have kids of his own, but he took on our crew like a pro. He settled us into our hotel on Tumon

Bay and left our jet-lagged selves to enjoy some sleep. Early the next morning, he showed up again in his van to give us a tour of the island, pointing out important sights. Sergeant Nick played tour guide and regaled us with facts and anecdotes about the area and experiences he'd had so far during his time in Guam. Our children delighted in his tales. Sergeant Nick seemed larger than life to them and brought a buzz of excitement to this strange new environment. Even three-year-old Anna bounced up and down in her car seat, heartily joining in the laughter at his stories and jokes that mostly went right over her head.

Nick also helped Steve with the multitude of tasks that go along with in-processing at a new duty station and put a human face on the logistics of the move for our whole family. He made those initial days of transition easier than they would have been otherwise. I won't ever forget his kindness and generosity, which eased our transition to life in Guam.

My grandparents had lived in Guam for a few years in the 1960s and had told stories about the island, but living there was still different from what I'd expected or ever experienced before. We all fell in love with the brilliant blue waters that surrounded the island. We learned to snorkel and spent many weekends exploring the coral reefs and playing on the pristine beaches, some of the most beautiful I've seen in my life. We took the kids to swim in the base pool most afternoons and spent weekends doing "boonie stomps," the name given to long walks and hikes through the surrounding jungle.

Shortly after we moved to Guam, we were invited to a village fiesta by one of Steve's civilian coworkers. Each village on the island, and there are many, celebrates its own patron saint yearly with regular fiestas. The whole island also celebrates various festivals together, which means there are fiestas going on nearly every weekend on the small island. When we arrived, we were immediately greeted as friends. We were ushered into a large, canopied area outdoors filled with crowds of people chatting, laughing, and eating. The smell of tropical flowers filled my senses, and I paused a moment to take in the sights as well. Long tables overflowed with food. Aunties in flowing floral dresses and sandals shooed away the children trying to sneak an early bite of the tempting feast. The children were playing and darting between family members, all laughing and talking together. In another tent, a group in long grass skirts performed a traditional Chamorro dance. My mouth watered as I took in the sight of juicy pineapple and mango, all manner of seafood, chunks of fresh coconut, the traditional Chamorro red rice, *lumpia, pancit*, spicy *finadene* sauce, and many dishes I couldn't identify yet. A crispy roasted pig, complete with an apple in its mouth, filled the center table. Our kids had never seen an entire roasted pig before. Six-year-old Grace pulled me aside to ask in a serious tone,

"Mom, did you see there's a whole pig up there? It has its face on and everything!" This was a lot of culture shock for one little girl, and she didn't eat meat for a while after that.

LESSONS OF LIFE OVERSEAS

No matter where you move overseas, there are adjustments to make. In Guam, I experienced island fever, feeling confined to a small island surrounded by thousands of miles of ocean. The pace of life there is much slower, which sounds kind of nice until it's time to renew your driver's license. On "island time," everything takes more time and more patience.

Time and patience are important when adjusting to any overseas assignment and a new culture. A bumper sticker I often saw while living in Hawaii read: "Slow down. This ain't the Mainland." It's good advice, whether in Guam or Germany or anywhere else. Most of the rest of the world doesn't operate on the same give-it-to-me-now hustle and bustle Americans are used to. When living in another country, everything from house-hunting, to setting up internet and cable service to auto repairs seems to take longer, require lots of paperwork and even more hoops to jump through. If military life teaches us to hurry up and wait, an overseas move raises the skill to an art form.

When you first move to a new country or culture, expect to feel more stupid than you ever have in your life as you deal with language barriers and different customs. You will feel like a fish out of water and have a moment or two of wishing you could go home, but I promise it will get better. These are some of the symptoms of culture shock, and the only cure is giving yourself time to adjust. Don't let it get you down, and don't give up.

Adjusting to life overseas isn't all inconvenience and homesickness, but it helps to know ahead of time that those elements are all part of the process. You'll also have many adventures and one-of-a-kind experiences. At some point, you'll look around and realize you're at home in this strange and wonderful place. You might be at a Chamorro festival, snorkeling in the waters of the Pacific, seeing the Alps for the first time, or sipping coffee at a German café. You'll pinch yourself and say, "I can't believe we get to live here!"

ROMAN HOLIDAY

"Aren't you even excited to see Michelangelo's *Moses* sculpture? What about *La Pietà*? And the Sistine Chapel?" enthused ten-year-old Anna, her pink marker poised over a list of museums and artwork she wanted to see on our trip to Rome.

I glanced in the rearview mirror to see her, our youngest, questioning our oldest, Matthew, who sat beside her on the minivan's middle seat. Matthew looked up from his phone.

"Oh my gosh, you are *such* a nerd," he said in a voice laced with boredom and annoyance.

Unfazed, Anna turned back to creating her checklist, marking her must-see sights with shiny Lisa Frank stickers.

I'd checked out a book from the base library about the art and history of Rome to prep the kids for our epic vacation. The large volume featured glossy photos of the masterpieces, architecture, and sculptures of the ancient city. Anna had taken our daily readings to heart and was enthralled with the possibility of seeing it all in person.

Like many military brats, our four children traveled more by the age of ten than their parents had by their early twenties. As we moved around the world, my husband and I made it a priority to introduce our children to the history, art, and culture within arm's reach at each assignment. In Germany, many other countries were within a few hours' drive, and we made the most of it.

On a trip to the Netherlands, we visited the Anne Frank house in Amsterdam, taking in the plight of a Jewish family in hiding from the Nazis during the Holocaust. In the countryside, we were amazed at the colorful tulips that spilled across seemingly endless fields. In Paris, we wandered through the Louvre, all of us surprised and fascinated with how small the *Mona Lisa* and her mysterious smile are in real life. Driving the backroads of Belgium, we paused in tiny villages for lunch or espresso on our way to peruse the wares of the *Bruges Zandfeesten*, or "Sand Festival," a huge flea market spanning blocks of the old city.

My husband and I felt lucky to be stationed in Europe with access to an abundance of living history and world-famous sights, and we assumed the kids would be as well. But after living there a few months, when we enthusiastically pointed out yet another beautiful landmark or monument, what we mostly got in return was a disinterested, "Oh look, *another* castle," from our not-so-easily-impressed offspring.

Teen attitudes notwithstanding, the whole family was excited about this vacation to Rome. We'd hoped to go in the fall but had to change our plans when Steve's deployment date was moved up. So, off we went in July, in full throttle vacation mode into the heat of the Italian summer.

Our tiny bed and breakfast in Rome, which had looked much roomier and more impressive online when I had booked it, was within a stone's throw of the Vatican. From one elf-sized window, we had a view of the neighbor's garden and the silhouette of Vatican City in the background—providing you could squeeze into the tiny balcony and open the shutter. If I squinted, I fancied I could also see the iconic Swiss Guard, the protectors of the pope and his city, clad in bright red, yellow, and blue.

Rome was one of those vacations in which time is precious and you don't want to waste a moment, so we started each day early; walked miles and miles to take in all the sights, sounds, and smells; and ended late in the evening in true Italian style.

In our travels we'd learned to plan for lots of breaks to avoid the whining that ensued partway into our walking tours—from me, not the kids. In Rome's summer heat, we often ducked into stores and bakeries to escape melting completely into the cobblestones.

Of course, many of the breaks we built into our days involved stopping for the cool, icy relief of a cup of gelato, which quickly became an intrinsic part of our sweaty Rome vacation. Everyone cranky from too many sights? Gelato! Would really rather take a nap, but there are still places to visit, and we only have a few more days to do it? Gelato! And of course, a long late dinner in Rome would be nothing if not capped off by, you guessed it, gelato!

Early on in our Roman holiday, Steve decided the Italian greeting, "*buongiorno*," or "good day" sounded an awful lot like the brand of our family's favorite frozen pizza.

"DiGiorno!" he would call enthusiastically at passers-by.

"Dad!" the kids would groan in embarrassment, and I would suddenly discover something very interesting in the window of a nearby shop, slide to the tail end of our group, and pretend I wasn't related to any of them.

We discovered a trattoria near our bed and breakfast and visited it nightly for our consumption of crispy, delicious pizza.

"DiGiorno!" Steve called, waving to the owner one evening as we walked in. Obviously, we were American tourists, but the owner was gracious. Perhaps he thought Steve was a bit dim, or maybe he had a sense of humor, the kind that appreciates a good dad joke in any language. I'd like to think it was the latter, as he seated us politely and stopped by our table throughout the evening to chat and laugh, often bringing extra drinks.

At the Colosseum, Steve shouted out "DiGiorno!" to the gladiator reenactors who posed outside, pestering tourists to snap photos with them—for a price. Steve's unexpected greeting startled them, and we scuttled past without being peppered by their aggressive sales pitch: "You want a photo, lady? You want a photo?"

I mean, a gladiator's gotta make a living somehow, I suppose, but I really did not want a photo. Or at least, not one I had to pay for.

The Facebook photos from our time in Rome show the laughable downward progression of my hairstyle each hot, steamy day—poofy in the morning, flat against my head by evening. The kids' expressions in those photos are also revealing: At the Colosseum, decked out with earphones and walkie-talkies for the tour narration, they look like my houseplants, wilting from what I like to call "cheerful neglect." In front of the ruins of Pompeii, part of a day trip to nearby Naples, the kids' forced smiles reflect their pleas for me to *Just stop taking photos and let us stand in the shade.* In front of St. Peter's Basilica, I and one child, who shall remain nameless, are sporting actual grimaces, a reaction to the constant—and often fruitless—search for a public toilet that is part of the European travel package. I think our eyes are watering, too. Let's just say, staying hydrated in Rome's heat did not mesh well with the lack of facilities.

But as family memories go, this was one for the books, and I did create an entire scrapbook dedicated to our Roman holiday. As I pasted the photos in, I relived the memories: gasping at our first sight of the Sistine Chapel, admiring sculptures by Bernini, sitting on the Spanish Steps, being wowed by the breathtaking view of the Castel Sant'Angelo at night, its lights reflected in the Tiber River. And yes, enjoying my daughter's delight when she finally saw *La Pietà* and *Moses.*

One remnant of our trip stands above it all, one of those silly moments that becomes part of a family's shared history and lexicon. Occasionally one of us still calls out, "DiGiornio!" with a smile or a laugh. It brings back a flood of memories: the masterpieces, the heat, the cool gelato, the crispy pizza, the ruins, the gladiators, and the cobblestone streets. And I just smile—perhaps a mysterious smile, like the *Mona Lisa*—except mine is bigger in real life.

CHOOSE YOUR ADVENTURE

In twenty-two years as an Army spouse, Tara and her husband, Dino, have raised four children and moved around the globe.

When Tara was growing up in Arizona, her dad had deployed with the National Guard. Military life wasn't completely unfamiliar, but certain aspects of life with an active-duty member would prove to be a surprise. After their marriage and the birth of their first child, Dino got orders to Germany. Until she traveled to Germany, Tara had never flown before.

"I was flying on a plane for the first time in my life with my eight-month-old baby girl. That was the craziest flight!"

She was excited to explore a different part of the world with her young husband and baby. But landing in a foreign country where she couldn't speak or understand the language, along with living in cramped military lodging for their first eight weeks in Germany, wasn't what she'd envisioned. Tara was at a loss for how to rebuild her life from scratch. The reality that she would not be returning home to live hit her hard.

"I cried every day for the first thirty days," she said. "I thought, *what have I done*? I missed my mom so much. I was only twenty. My husband wondered if he was going to have to send me back home."

Tara said she knew she had to make it work. Going home and leaving her husband behind wasn't a realistic option. Over time, she began to meet other spouses in the same situation and started to make friends. Together they ventured off the Army post to explore the local villages and countryside.

"One thing I realized about friendships at overseas bases is that we just need each other so much. When we first moved back to the U.S., I thought people were unfriendly where we were stationed. I didn't put it together then that it was simply the difference between overseas and a stateside assignment. Everyone sticks together over there."

Years later, Dino had an opportunity to be stationed back near Tara's hometown.

"I was sitting nearby while he was on the phone with his work, waiting to hear the news of his next assignment. I kept praying, 'Ok, Jesus, come on, Arizona, Arizona, Arizona!'"

Dino, listening intently to the person on the other end of the phone, silently penned out "Japan" on a scrap of paper for Tara to see. She immediately shifted gears, and said, "Take it!"

"The funny thing is, I had really wanted to go home," said Tara. "Even though it had been years since I lived there, I'd been really missing it. But when he wrote down 'Japan,' I switched to, 'Let's go on an adventure!'"

The couple, now with four children, moved over the ocean and back six times, living in Germany, Okinawa, and Korea.

Reflecting on her decades of military life, Tara said she's grateful for her experiences, the friends she made, and how she found the strength to embrace whatever came.

WEATHERING THE STORMS

I pulled the blanket over my shoulder, wedged myself up on my pillow, slid the laptop closer to me on the bed, and settled in for a wakeful night. I'd be on tsunami watch for the coming hours.

Earlier in the evening, I'd had a call from Steve, who was in DC on temporary duty.

"You're under a tsunami warning, babe," he said. A hint of urgency in his voice let me know he was concerned, and that concerned me. He didn't worry about much and was always the calm, pragmatic counterpart to my anxious, worst-case-scenario energy. But an 8.8 magnitude earthquake had hit Chile, across the wide Pacific Ocean in South America, and it looked like a dangerous tidal wave—a tsunami—had been triggered and could be headed in our direction.

"Um, so what exactly do I *do*?" I asked him. Tsunamis were not a situation I was prepared for. Our home was right along the shore of the entrance to historic Pearl Harbor. We all remembered the death and destruction that had occurred in the terrible Indian Ocean tsunami just a few years before, and my mind churned with thoughts of getting the kids, our dog, and some essential belongings to higher ground . . . *where*, exactly?

Steve assured me that, should the decision be made to evacuate the base, we'd be given plenty of notice and told all the information we'd need. I was still worried.

That's some comfort, I thought darkly. *So, I just sit here and wait?*

I wandered out to the front yard, thinking through scenarios and possibilities. The island of Oahu is only about forty by thirty miles in size, and I wondered if a tsunami such as the disastrous one in the Indian Ocean in 2004 could cover the island completely. Maybe not, I mused, since Oahu has two large mountain ranges.

"Jen!" A voice shook me from my dark thoughts, and I looked up to see my neighbor Maria hurrying toward me.

She'd just heard the news from her husband—who also happened to be TDY. (Remember what I said about Murphy's Law?) Maria no longer had kids at home, but she was a dog mom to two large pups she'd need to bring with her if we evacuated. We compared notes on what little we knew, and each promised we wouldn't evacuate without the other. So now here I lay, watching the live webcam streaming from Waikiki Beach, wondering if we should play it safe and head further inland now. But the kids were all asleep, and our little dog Toby was curled up by my feet. Our bags were packed with a few necessities and sitting by the door. It seemed there was nothing to do now but wait.

After a fitful night of checking and re-checking that my phone was set to notify me of emergency alerts, dozing off then startling awake to check the news and beach webcam, and bracing myself for a knock on the door that meant *get out now*, I finally fell asleep around four in the morning and slept a few uneasy hours. The next day brought good news. The wave had been reduced to the tiniest blip by the time it reached us. The live streams had barely even registered a ripple. *Thank God.* What could have been a life-altering event turned out to be nothing, but that wasn't always the case.

As I mentioned before, we have a running joke in our family that weird weather events followed us around the world. We were in Ohio for the "Storm of the Century" in 1993 that dumped feet of snow across the country and shut down large swathes of the Eastern Seaboard.

While we lived in Florida, we experienced many tropical storms and hurricane warnings. During one particularly bad storm, we watched the water rise to our porch steps, gently lapping the top step as if considering its next move. It threatened to spill into our base housing but stopped short of our threshold. I cursed the "powers that be" for not instructing housing residents to leave, because now we were stuck in our homes until the water receded completely. The flooding deluged our storage unit, ruining keepsakes and wedding mementos. Still, we were thankful that those losses and a few downed trees were all we suffered.

In Germany, a freak windstorm tossed our tied down trampoline into the air and over the fence, bending it in half like a warmed tortilla. And when we were moving from our house on Joint Base Anacostia-Bolling in Washington, DC, Hurricane Sandy hit the East Coast right after our household goods had been loaded onto a moving truck.

The storms of life, indeed.

SHAKEN AND STIRRED

By far, the worst natural disasters we encountered were in Guam. Shortly after our arrival in 2002, we were awakened by a noise I can only describe as hundreds of trains traveling beneath our house. Half asleep, I struggled to make sense of what was happening. We heard cabinet doors slamming open and glass shattering as pictures fell off the wall and glassware flew from the shelves. The house's emergency lights kicked on as the power went out. I could see Steve repeatedly struggling to stand up, trying to get to the kids, and falling down again. I attempted to get out of bed, too, but another jolt slammed me into the dresser. Flat on the carpet, I could hear myself gasping for breath. Forcing myself not to panic, I pulled myself to the doorway and saw my three-year-old on her belly, making a determined Marine crawl toward me, her blankie clutched in one little hand. Then, as suddenly as it began, it was over.

"Mom, Dad? What was *that*?" said a little voice from the boys' room.

We'd been warned about earthquakes in that part of the world, but we'd never experienced one, and we've certainly never felt one that strong again. We learned later it was measured at 7.1 magnitude. Surprisingly, our house didn't sustain any major damage, but for days we experienced aftershocks and I'd instinctively grab a wall or a nearby person. Even months later when we felt a tremor, I'd reach for anything solid. I never did get used to earthquakes.

In December of that same year, we watched as Super Typhoon Pongsona bore down on our tiny island. I fielded calls from extended family back in the States about the storm coming our way. I knew it had to be bad if they'd heard about it. Though Guam is a U.S. territory, it seemed most Americans had no idea it existed, let alone paid attention to its weather reports.

Typhoons and hurricanes, by the way, are the same type of storm: tropical cyclones. The only difference is terminology. A tropical cyclone in the Northwest Pacific is called a typhoon. In the North Atlantic, central North Pacific, and eastern North Pacific, it's called a hurricane.[2] A super typhoon is the same as a Category 5 hurricane, indicating sustained winds of around 150 miles per hour and above.[3]

In the hurricane part of the world, we'd lived through plenty of Florida's tropical storms. Plus, we'd already experienced back-to-back typhoons in Guam just six months earlier (during which my husband cheerfully enthused, "How many people get to say they've gone through two typhoons in *one week*?") We knew what supplies to have on hand and had purchased a generator to get us through the power outage that would inevitably follow this storm.

Though we felt prepared, we knew the prospect of a super typhoon was no joke. During a phone call with my mom, I kept one eye on the television weather radar and tried to keep the conversation upbeat. However, my stomach clenched as I looked at images of the huge storm and its distinctly formed eye, rolling across the Pacific on a direct track to Guam.

"Where will you go?" Mom asked worriedly. I laughed it off. We wouldn't go anywhere. Typhoon procedure for military families stationed in Guam was to hunker down and see it through. I assured her we'd be fine, *just fine*, and would ride out the storm in our bunker-like concrete house with its steel doors and storm shutters. When I got off the phone, Steve told me the military was indeed offering to evacuate families to Hawaii. However, he would not be going, as all active-duty members were required to stay put for the duration. In my mind, there was no question. No way was I leaving him behind while I lolled around in comfort on a beach in Hawaii. Over the next day, the base's flightline hummed as pilots moved aircraft to safety at bases in nearby countries.

So, we heaved all the metal shutters closed, stowed away all the outside play gear, tied down what wouldn't fit in the house or storage unit, and opened up our "typhoon closet." The military instructs families stationed in Guam to stock up on certain items in preparation for typhoons—battery operated fans and lamps, nonperishable food, plenty of bottled water, and of course, batteries. Our typhoon plans also included cards, books, and board games. Through the long hours, we kept the children occupied as the storm slammed into the island with sustained winds of over 140 miles per hour and gusts exceeding 170.[4] We winced at the sounds of trees falling on houses and cars and parts of buildings being ripped away. One loud crack made us all jump when a palm tree crashed into the storage area attached to our house.

Hours later, long after our power had gone out, there was a sudden, eerie silence. We knew we were experiencing a short reprieve as the eye of the storm passed over us. Steve popped the door open a few inches to look out, and seeing neighbors do the same thing, ventured outside to assess damages and compare notes for a few moments.

Relieved that our home was still intact, I stepped out onto the front porch and took in the eerie landscape. Trees lay scattered like matchsticks across yards, roofs, and streets. A roof was blown off of a nearby house. A bare concrete slab was all that remained of a storage unit at our neighbor's house. The most shocking sight to me was that every leaf was gone from every tree. It was apocalyptic. The bare palm trees that were left standing looked like sticks a giant had haphazardly stuck into the ground.

One spot of normalcy in the shattered landscape was a circle of neighborhood men standing in the quintessential "dad stance," feet spread and hands on hips, discussing the damage and upcoming clean-up. I gulped and held back tears as we headed back inside to brace ourselves for the opposite eyewall of the typhoon passing over us. If the base had sustained this much damage with our reinforced homes, I could only imagine what those living off base were going through.

AFTERMATH

After the storm, we learned our generator would be useless. Gasoline was in short supply, because the main gasoline tanks off base were set on fire by a lightning strike during the storm. We'd been so sure we were prepared and would sail through this storm's aftermath. Instead, we'd be without power and running water for the next couple of weeks, along with everyone else across the island. It took months for power to be restored to some remote areas. Many of us from the base became involved with relief work off base, which gave us some perspective. Damages to thousands of civilian homes and businesses across the island totaled millions of dollars. Hundreds of injuries and one death were attributed to the storm.[5]

Over the coming weeks, the military supplied rations of water and staples for us. I felt like a pioneer woman, washing out our clothing on a Lego table with a few drips from a jug of water and rationed detergent. Necessity is indeed the mother of invention. Without power and air conditioning, we quickly realized a concrete bunker house is great for storm protection, but not so great for airflow. The carpets and furniture began to take on a squishy factor and all of us began to smell a little, well—funky.

The kids seemed to consider all this a grand adventure. Families were invited to eat meals at the base's chow hall, which had generator power. Our kids loved meeting up with neighbors and friends at mealtime and choosing actual food from the chow hall line, instead of the Fruit Roll-Ups and SpaghettiOs we were rationing at home. They also reveled in wearing the same clothes several days in a row. They were kids, after all. We joined neighbors to clear debris, trees, and palm fronds, and the kids loved taking breaks from the clean-up efforts to play with their friends in the neighborhood. In fact, they weren't unhappy at all.

When I was tempted to feel grouchy at the heat, humidity, and inconvenience, I'd just watch my children laughing and playing and learn from their example. And I was thankful it wasn't worse.

All these storms, typhoons, threatened tsunamis, blizzards, earthquakes, and power and water outages were more reminders that we don't have much control over our lives. We can only control how we react. A little flexibility—the fine art of "Semper Gumby"—means I can bend rather than break. I can't control the weather, but I control how I weather the storm. That part is up to me. And I learned it from my kids.

HAWAII AND BACK AGAIN

As well as storms, we also had some great vacations while stationed in Guam. One of our most unforgettable family trips during those years was a vacation to Australia. Knowing we were closer in Guam to being Down Under than we'd probably ever be again, we snapped up a discounted vacation package and spent a week there, enjoying experiences like riding a tram high above the dense rainforest, taking a catamaran adventure, and snorkeling the Great Barrier Reef. When it came time to return home, our kids were reluctant to leave. Our second son, Gabriel, was a huge fan of Steve Irwin, star of *The Crocodile Hunter*, and was upset that the Air Force couldn't see fit to move us to the country of his hero.

I found my dream location on another trip we took while stationed in Guam. We had the opportunity to travel for free on a space-available military flight to Oahu in Hawaii.

Our children were young, and we were all excited to have a week to enjoy Hawaii's beautiful beaches and mountains. After the surprisingly cold and bumpy flight—it was a military cargo plane, after all—we arrived at Joint Base Pearl Harbor-Hickam, picked up our rental car, and drove across the island on Interstate H-3 on our way to stay at Bellows Air Force Station on the windward side of the island. The highway winds through the beautiful and other-worldly Koʻolau Mountains. Water flowed from waterfalls dotted here and there high on the mountains. Lush green trees and thick plants gave us the sense that we'd stepped into the jungles of *Jurassic Park*. As we crested the top of one mountain, I spotted the crystal turquoise waters of the Pacific shimmering off the coast. I was in awe of the panorama, as though we'd stepped onto another planet completely.

"I cannot believe how beautiful this is," I said to Steve. "Do you think we could ever get stationed here?"

He agreed it was gorgeous but answered, "Babe, *everyone* wants to get stationed here, so don't get your hopes up."

Yet, some dreams do come true. A few assignments later, when Steve had just returned from a deployment to Afghanistan, he received orders to Joint Base Pearl Harbor-Hickam. By that point, our oldest was in his first year of college, and between the highs and lows of leaving behind our first child at his school in Texas and the reintegration transition after Steve's deployment, the beauty of Hawaii soothed me again with its peacefulness. I felt a connection to the surroundings that I hadn't felt since I'd left the mountains in my home state of New Mexico. In Hawaii, I'd often walk for miles along the bike and jogging path that ran behind Hickam at the entrance to Pearl Harbor, thinking and praying. When I'd walk the same path at sunset, the sun glowing across the water before it slipped out of sight, a calm would enfold me and remind me to drink in these moments. I often thought, *I could live here forever.*

I HAVE SOMETHING TO TELL YOU

We'd been at our dream duty station for a grand total of three months when we received our household goods shipment. Our belongings had taken their sweet time wending their way from Germany to Oahu, across both the Atlantic and Pacific Oceans as well as traversing the continental U.S. It was like Christmas morning when they arrived as we opened boxes and spotted our familiar things.

The kids were already busy with schoolwork and new-found friends and sports practices. I homeschooled and worked from home, so, as was normally the case, the bulk of the tasks of unpacking and creating a new home fell to me. I always reveled in this task, setting out the familiar knick-knacks and hanging family photos. Each piece put in its rightful spot brought a sense of home and normality.

One afternoon I was hanging the last of the curtains, perched on a wobbly step stool in our base house when I heard the door open. On tiptoe, stretching my full height to attach the final curtain hook, I turned my head and was surprised to see my husband home from work at three o'clock on a Tuesday. Maybe he'd forgotten some paperwork or was running by on his way to some ceremony or other.

"You might want to stop doing that, babe," he said. I did not like the look on his face. "I have something to tell you."

I plopped down on the top of the step stool and sighed. In military life, "I have something to tell you" is rarely followed by welcome news. But it couldn't be another deployment. Steve had recently returned from a year in Afghanistan. He'd only come home a week before we made the move from Germany to Hawaii, so he should be staying put for a while. It couldn't be PCS orders, because we'd just moved, hence my curtain hanging. No, it couldn't be that.

But it was. It turned out that the "powers that be" (that far off, nebulous group I liked to blame for any weird happenings in military life) had decided to deactivate the unit where Steve had recently become the command chief, head of all enlisted personnel. He'd been interviewed and chosen from a slate of candidates for this position. It was a step up, a milestone, a great thing for his career. How could this be? Was this a sudden decision, or had those "powers that be" known all along and moved our family across the world anyway? I'll never know, but it was decided. The unit would be absorbed into another organization, and with the change Steve's position would simply go away. Chalk it up as one of the many inexplicable events of military life.

I was devastated. We'd gratefully received the welcome baskets when we'd arrived, taken the newcomers' tour of the base, and explored the island and made lists of all the places we wanted to visit and restaurants we'd try. Even though we'd only been there a handful of months, I was already plugged into the spouse club, and the kids were making friends. We were *all in* for this Hawaii life. One daughter was already playing competitive volleyball with a club off base, and our youngest had joined a musical theater group. We'd found a church, and we loved the beach life.

"*Well, too darn bad,*" the Air Force seemed to say. "*You're at our mercy.*"

My dream of living in Hawaii forever was not to be. Instead, we were on the move again, this time to Washington, DC, and a new assignment for Steve at the Pentagon. As our plane lifted off from Honolulu, I plastered my face against the plane window. Tears ran down my cheeks as I watched the beautiful island and the sight of Diamond Head recede, mourning that our time in paradise had been cut short.

After we arrived in DC, we did our best to make the most of it and embrace the opportunities that come with living in the National Capital Region. We planned a different adventure each weekend, as we knew this would be a short assignment for Steve. We made a list of all the must-see locations we didn't want to miss: the Smithsonian, Mount Vernon, the monuments, the trails, the museums. I learned to navigate DC traffic, and the kids plugged into new communities yet again.

Sometimes dreams get delayed, and that was the case for my dreams of Hawaii. One year later we boarded a plane headed back to Hawaii, where Steve would become the Command Chief Master Sergeant for Pacific Air Forces, leading a total enlisted force of over 40,000 airmen across the Pacific. I was happy for this great opportunity for him, of course, but even happier for *me* that I would be returning to my Hawaiian adventure. Sometimes, life works out and you get another chance. I was thrilled to pick up my island life again and spend another two years on the beautiful island of Oahu.

NOT GOING BACK TO SCHOOL

My middle-school daughter plunged—with uneven amounts of volume and skill—into her fifth rendition of Beethoven's "Für Elise" on our battered piano. At the kitchen counter, my oldest son peered into a microscope, attempting to sketch protozoa in his lab book, stopping occasionally to complain about his sister's piano-playing.

"Mom, can you please make her stop?" he pleaded.

My other son lounged in the recliner, engrossed in his latest *Hank the Cowdog* book and oblivious to the commotion. My youngest daughter sprawled happily on the couch, swinging her legs and eating cookies while sounding out words from her phonics cards. The dog stayed close to her, knowing she was a source of frequent pats on the head and, possibly, errant cookie crumbs.

Moms with children of differing ages can likely relate to this busy family scenario on afternoons or weekends, but this was a regular school day for our homeschool family.

I never planned to be a homeschooler.

In fact, if you'd told me before we had kids that I would not only homeschool our four children but keep at it for years and years, I would've probably laughed hysterically or fled in the other direction. The only homeschooling families I'd run across before were a bit—let's say "different." So why did we decide to homeschool as a military family?

It was the combination of our oldest child learning to read early, a desire for a faith-based education without the finances for private school, and that we'd encountered several families who'd successfully homeschooled for years that led us to consider this option when our oldest reached school age. We decided to try it for one year. To my surprise, we'd had an absolute ball, as he learned reading and writing basics and we spent oodles of time outdoors and took field trips with a local homeschooling group. He soaked it all in like a sponge. Taking complete responsibility for your child's education would not be defined as *easy*, but we found that the flexibility of homeschooling seamlessly fit our busy military life. As more children came along and the moves ticked up, we continued homeschooling. It provided continuity in our kids' education. We didn't need to worry about school districts when deciding where to live in a new place.

I am by no means a homeschooling purist who thinks it's the only way to educate children—or even that it's the best decision for every family. But as I look back over the years, I'm convinced it was the right choice for us. As we moved around the world, homeschooling took on many different iterations for us: co-ops, charter schools, dual enrollment, enrichment classes, and more. We partnered with some lovely teachers and schooling situations to create what we hoped was the best experience for our kiddos. I loved that we had so many educational choices and could select what worked best for our family.

Another benefit of homeschooling was the freedom it gave us to travel during the off season or have the flexibility to take a break when Steve took leave or came home for R&R during deployments. It was also beneficial when our moves happened during the regular school year. We could pick up and move at any time to any location with our portable school, since we set our own school calendar.

Army wife Crystal Niehoff, host of the *Military Homeschool Podcast*, said this is one of many benefits of homeschooling for military families. Another is continuity from one duty station to the next.

"Homeschooling gives my kids the stability and consistency they need to survive or even thrive in military life, as it's always changing," she said. "We can take a break when we need to for PCS moves or deployments, no big deal. We can travel to see family when airfare is cheaper, and go to Disney when everyone else is in school and the lines are shorter! For me, the biggest benefit is that I don't have to worry about them falling behind or struggling with each new school."

IS THAT LEGAL?

Despite the many benefits, friends and extended family have often expressed common concerns about our choice to homeschool our children. I've frequently encountered the same questions and fears from skeptics and from parents considering home education. Here are a few.

Is homeschooling legal? Yes, in all fifty states and U.S. Territories. Overseas, military families fall under Status of Forces Agreements between the U.S. and host countries and aren't bound by local educational laws like those in Germany, where homeschooling is illegal for its own population. The Department of Defense Education Activity (DoDEA), which oversees overseas schools for military-connected students, has a policy of neither encouraging nor discouraging homeschooling. Homeschoolers can take advantage of many DoDEA benefits. During our time stationed in numerous states and countries, the only time we ever had a legal issue was with a local school district in North Dakota. The district wanted to send a teacher to regularly "observe" our homeschooling. Fortunately, we were members of Home School Legal Defense Association, which advocated on our behalf and informed the school district they could not require any supervision of our homeschool.

How will your children make friends and become socialized? Won't they become weird little hermits? Well, maybe. But honestly, that's probably more to do with personality than schooling choices. Homeschooling is no longer rare, and opportunities for connection have exploded. We found far more enrichment and educational activities than most children have time to attend—and plenty of opportunities for socialization. Even the most remote bases we've been assigned to have organized homeschooling groups and activities.

I'm not patient enough to homeschool. This one always cracks me up, and to that I say, "Me neither!" If you're under the impression that being a homeschooling parent requires perfection, please drop that notion right now. One truth about homeschooling is that your kids will see you day in and day out, warts and all. It's taught me plenty of humility and the fine art of apologizing to my kids when necessary.

I'm not qualified to teach _____ (Fill in the blank with any subject or grade level.) Again: Me neither! Homeschooling doesn't mean the parent has to be an expert in everything. If there are subjects you don't feel you can teach, there are loads of resources at your disposal. Living in the technology era has its benefits: From online Algebra classes—hallelujah! —to dual enrollment in your local school, there are numerous options to assist the teaching parent. As each of our children reached high school, I became more of an academic adviser, guiding them in their chosen courses rather than directly teaching each subject.

Can I homeschool if I'm a working parent? It's certainly more challenging to work and homeschool, but it's not impossible. I've known several families who've managed their work schedule around homeschooling. Personally, I was a work-from-home mom during our last five years or so of homeschooling and I juggled outside volunteer responsibilities as well. It can be done.

Will my child be prepared for college and adult life if we homeschool? Yes! Our homeschool graduates have won scholarships, adapted well to the independent study required for college life, and even joined the military. There is much evidence that home education prepares students with the independence and study skills required for the college environment.

Each of our now grown children had very different interest growing up: varsity sports, guitar, piano, drumline, Irish dance, youth performing arts, graphic arts, and photography. One of our family mottos was: "We don't homeschool to close doors for our children, but to open them." For us, there was nothing better than the flexibility, uniqueness, and fun of homeschooling. Even when my two youngest children reached high-school age, we enjoyed reading aloud together each morning. It was one of our favorite things, and we covered hundreds of books that way.

Whatever educational choices you make—homeschool, public, or private school—you can change course if it doesn't work for you. If you're looking for a different path for your family, live in a remote location, or are simply curious about homeschooling, I encourage you to consider it. It was a wonderful experience for our family.

WHAT ABOUT ME?

My husband flipped me a small yellow business card.

"They're looking for a blog editor," he remarked casually, "and I told them you'd be perfect."

"Huh?"

I looked up from where I'd been packing up my toiletries in our temporary lodging room at Joint Base Langley-Eustis in Virginia. I was only half listening as he went on to talk about meeting a retired Marine Corps couple at a military conference he'd just attended. They'd seemed like a nice, friendly couple, he said. They owned a business and were looking for help with their online content. We'd just arrived from Hawaii a few weeks earlier and were due to move into our new house on base at Langley in a couple of days. I was eyeball deep, swamped by that "too many things on my to-do list" state. I glanced briefly at the card and stuffed it into my laptop bag. I didn't have the mental capacity to think about new jobs, as I coordinated with movers and made plans to get settled into our new home quickly. And I had a sneaking suspicion the nice couple might have been humoring him just a wee bit. I truly appreciate Steve being my biggest fan, but he tends to be a little overly enthusiastic about me and likely had gone a bit over the top when talking about my abilities.

I'd left a position as a managing editor of a magazine when we left Hawaii. It was a stressful role and a fast-paced work environment. Frankly, I was ready for a break—then. But weeks later, settled into the latest new house with little to do, time weighed heavily on me. On the surface, I stayed occupied. I was homeschooling our youngest daughter, Anna, the last child still in school. She was a senior in high school, and we'd joined a local homeschooling co-op, so she could complete her final credits and be part of a group graduation. At this point, I was more coach than teacher, cheering her on and overseeing her classes. I enjoyed being involved with the military community and volunteering, but I felt like I was missing a purpose. A paycheck would be nice, too.

A couple of months later, when I finally got around to emptying my laptop bag, the bright yellow card fell out with a pile of other papers. The yellow caught my eye. It said, "Military-ByOwner Advertising, Contact Sharon." I looked at the email and phone and wondered. I doubted the position was still open, but I took a chance and sent an email. To my surprise, I was invited to a video job interview that very week. Turns out, they did still need someone to fill that position, and they were interested. We hit it off in that first video interview, and I've been with the company ever since. Sometimes good things drop into your lap because of a husband's enthusiasm.

In fact, Steve was my biggest support when I'd made the decision to seriously pursue writing when we were in Hawaii. I'd dabbled in freelance writing over the years, but after dropping our oldest off at college before that move, I'd realized it was time to get serious. I enrolled in some writing and editing courses while we were in lodging in Hawaii for several months, waiting for a house.

A couple of weeks after we moved into our Hawaii home, the front door swung open, and Steve wrestled a piece of furniture into our front room.

"This is *mom's* desk," he said to our three teenagers still at home. "If you see her here working on something, you're not to bother her." I was stunned by his pronouncement but so grateful. I spent countless hours sitting at that desk, honing my skills, studying writing and grammar manuals. I plowed away at writing, writing, and more writing, I would stay up too late tweaking sentences, sending numerous submissions to magazines—some rejected, some published— and finally got my first actual payment for a published work. I eventually landed a part-time gig writing reviews for a magazine. It was the start of my second career, one that I'd dreamed of having for years but which seemed unrealistic and too far out of reach. I'd been out of the workforce for some years and had some trepidation about attempting a career as a writer. It was a far cry from my nursing days, a career I wasn't eager to go back to after so many years out of the field. Like so many military spouses, I pivoted to a new career.

Surveys on military spouse employment show that many military spouses are underemployed. In other words: overqualified. They have more formal education and experience than is required at their current or most recent work position. There's also a continued income gap between armed forces spouses and their civilian counterparts.[6]

This is no surprise to most military spouses. We've been there: moving to a new area, combing online ads, sending in resumes, and applying for jobs that aren't really a fit. But something is better than nothing. I've often addressed this topic with guests on my *Milspouse Matters* podcast. It's a common theme for military spouses.

At one of my first job interviews as a military spouse, I was asked: "What brings you to the area?" Followed quickly by, "How long will you be here?" I hemmed and hawed my way through that interview, didn't give a straight answer to the second question, and (surprisingly) landed the job.

A friend of mine confessed that she's straight-out lied at job interviews about how long she'll be in an area. After being passed over for opportunities several times, she's also learned to avoid any mention of her husband's military service. Mobility is not exclusive to the military, of course. Our society is more mobile than ever, so frequent moves are not rare as they once were. And have you ever considered that the strength and flexibility you've developed as a military spouse may be to your advantage?

THE MOTHER OF REINVENTION

Over the years, my role has shifted from nurse to new mom to homeschooling stay-at-home-mom to writer, editor, and pod-caster. Now I'm an empty nester who's busier than ever. This changing of jobs, careers, and even focus is familiar to military spouses who struggle to balance the demands of military life with their own career aspirations. Those of us who once swore we'd never stay home with kids or give up our professional identity end up doing just that, even if only for a season.

It can be singularly frustrating to leave a great job and start all over at a new location. Spouses may struggle to find a new position, or they may have to start all over at the bottom of the ladder of a new company. Others face childcare issues while juggling schedules with a spouse who's deployed or working night shifts. In light of how military life impacts the entire family, some spouses find the stress of holding down a job isn't worth the headache or cost of childcare.

A few years back, I read an article that suggested that there were twice the number of stay-at-home moms in the military community than in the civilian population. My admittedly unscientific observations have borne this out. Many military families make the decision to have one parent stay home or work from home to provide stability and care for the children, others stay home temporarily while waiting for professional licensure to transfer, while some find themselves unable to find work in their chosen field, especially when they're at a remote or overseas location. Status of Forces Agreements with some countries don't allow military family members to take jobs on the local economy. So many military spouses re-invent themselves, or like I did, pursue second careers or re-mote work. Others delve into the world of volunteerism.

Much has been written about what military spouses give up professionally to follow their loved ones around the globe.

Tireless advocacy has brought a greater awareness of military spouse employment issues and some important changes. The Military Spouse Licensing Relief Act of 2021 was passed by Congress to help spouses transfer professional licenses when moving on military orders from state to state.[7] The Military Spouse Employment Act was passed in 2023 to give spouses an edge when applying for jobs with federal agencies. I hope all this is creating a better job landscape for all of us.[8]

Despite the progress made, spouses still must navigate the reality of leaving behind jobs and interests because the military says it's time to move on. Legislation and awareness don't fix every problem.

"Careers which require professional licensure are especially challenging," said military spouse Stephanie. We work hard to get our degrees, experience, and knowledge. My advice: don't give up. Push through the red tape and be flexible."

Air Force wife Angela has determined to focus on the positive side of job and career changes. She looks for new short-term careers with each move, creating her own kind of success.

"I get to reinvent myself and try out new things," she said. "Perhaps, someday, I'll get to choose one and stick with it."

Ashley said she looks for flexibility. "Not planning my life around my job has become key, as our family is Navy and goes through months every year with my spouse at sea. Loving what you do also makes a huge difference! Be flexible and prepared to accept changes in your career path."

Other military spouses spoke of filling their time with volunteering at duty stations where they were unable to find work, often in a field they're already interested in or one they wanted to explore. Even when it's not their first choice, finding a positive way forward is important.

"If you're at a duty station where jobs are limited, volunteer," said Army spouse Josie. "It's valuable experience that can be put on a resume. You'll also make new friends, and maybe find an interest you might not have otherwise."

All of this advice, of course, reflects the truth for military spouses and their careers. They usually have to bend to fit the facts of military life.

"What about me?" we may wonder. "When do I get to come first?"

It's a dilemma most women grapple with at some point, as they balance marriage, motherhood, and career. The demands of military life add several degrees of difficulty to that balancing act for spouses. My personal belief that God is in control informs all the decisions I make for the sake of my family, along with the simple belief that everything happens for a reason. These foundational principles give me the wisdom not to project too far forward, because I'm not very good at guessing what's coming next anyway.

Being a military spouse has not kept me from growing and learning. Who I am today is a far cry from the young spouse I was thirty years ago. I couldn't have imagined—as I made career sacrifices and experienced years of low or no pay—the opportunities that would come later. I also didn't know then how much I would appreciate being at home with my children through those years. I leaned into homey tasks like cooking, baking, sewing. I enjoyed the little moments of reading with our children and simply being *all in* for them.

When I began to take on work-from-home jobs, while our family was still active duty, I realized I couldn't do it all. I had to set limits. Sometimes, the opportunities I felt I missed because of military life or family needs seemed like difficult sacrifices. Later, I had even greater opportunities for experiences and jobs I couldn't have dreamed up myself. When I had to work extra in the evenings or on a weekend as I pursued my burgeoning second career as a writer, my children were witness to me pursuing my own dreams. When I've had to leave them to attend professional conferences and events; when I've felt overwhelmed with a pile of work and the stress of military life, and when I've celebrated the good moments, my children saw my real life and the work in progress that I am, and we all are.

What about me? This is a legitimate question, especially for a military spouse wondering what's ahead. There's more than one answer to that question, and it may be different depending on what season you are in. I've become a firm believer in the concept of "seasons of life," and have truly seen this play out in my own life. In some seasons, the needs of the military and family come first, and in other seasons, we get opportunities we never expected. But we don't have to figure it all out today. There are more seasons to come.

SNOWBLOWERS AND SUNFLOWERS

At first, news of Steve's assignment to North Dakota felt like some form of karma—payback for the preceding assignments we'd spent in the warmth of Guam and Florida. We'd discovered we were beach people and thrived in the sunshine and surf. In fact, it had been so long since we'd lived somewhere requiring more than shorts and swimsuits, none of the kids had appropriate winter attire. They had outgrown it all. My sister-in-law Teri back in the States ran to thrift stores for us and kindly sent us a box of used jackets to have on hand when we arrived. Thank God. Landing in North Dakota in April, we'd thought we'd be in the "warming up" part of the year, but thirty degrees Fahrenheit was a cold and rude awakening after leaving island life.

After we landed at the tiny Grand Forks airport and were dropped off at base lodging, Steve got on the phone to deal with rental car issues. The kids and I walked to the commissary a couple of blocks away to grab breakfast staples for the next morning. We huddled together as we walked, shivering and exhausted from the long plane trip. Anna lagged a few steps behind, expressing all our feelings with her cry, "Why is it so c-c-c-cold?"

Spring did finally arrive, and then summer. As our spirits thawed along with the landscape, fields of huge sunflowers pushed up through the previously frozen ground. It was time to embrace this new life and see what it had to offer. We drove to South Dakota and took in the wonders of the Black Hills, the Badlands, and Mount Rushmore. We stopped for tractors on the highway and became acclimated to life in farm country. We picked juicy strawberries from the black dirt. We found a church, and the kids jumped into new friendships. No matter how long or hard the winter is, spring always comes.

Change is never easy, is it? As military families, we often move away from familiar faces and places, starting over again and again. Sometimes it doesn't seem worth the effort when we know that the new community and friendships will likely be temporary. It's a conscious choice to plug into a new location yet another time, to connect when we know the hurt that awaits with the inevitable goodbyes.

Just as we welcomed the sight of the sunflowers, we learned to appreciate the snow.

"Anna! Grace!" I opened the frosty storm door to call out. "Where are you girls?"

Two brightly hooded heads popped up from different parts of the snow-covered yard like a cute game of Whack-a-Mole. Red-cheeked, the girls giggled in delight at having tricked me.

"We're making a snow tunnel!" Grace called back.

Shivering, I waved and reminded them that they'd need to come back inside in about ten minutes to warm up for a bit, then returned to the cocoon of my warm home. Winter had come, and the temperature hovered right about zero. That day it had "warmed up" enough from the twenty-below temps of the preceding days, so I'd allowed the girls to go outside and play. The children created a maze of tunnels through the deep snow that covered our yard at Grand Forks Air Force Base, North Dakota, and spent hours in their make-believe world. Once, as a friend arrived for dinner one quiet winter evening, the kids popped up suddenly from under a layer of seemingly undisturbed snow and scared his pants off.

As the snow accumulated during our first winter in the "frozen tundra," as I not-so-fondly referred to it, Steve and the kids piled up a massive snow hill next to the house, nearly to the height of the second story. Someone, likely my husband, came up with the genius idea of pouring water out the window over the hill, which immediately froze and became a slick path to ride down on their plastic snow saucers.

I had not looked forward to the cold winters of North Dakota before we moved there, but there were some things about the climate and place that I found intriguing. One was the dump trucks that hauled the huge mounds of snow left by the snowplows. The trucks carted the snow away every few days to deposit it in empty parking lots and fields, creating massive glaciers that took weeks to melt off in the springtime. The sight of snow, snow everywhere, wasn't something I really ever became accustomed to.

In Grand Forks, it started snowing in October and didn't completely melt off until April or May. And digging out from a new snowfall could take some time. One winter Saturday morning, I'd volunteered to work at a spouse club pancake breakfast fundraiser. With Steve deployed, of course, I'd allowed what I thought was enough time to clear the driveway from the previous night's snowstorm. I hit the button to raise the garage door and stood and watched as the door slowly rose revealing nothing but snow as the door went up. When it reached the point that the snow drift was taller than my head, I smacked the button again to close it. I knew it would take me at least an hour to clear it all, and by then I'd miss my volunteer shift anyway.

Battling the constant snow became part of my new winter workout routine. After spending exhausting hours at the beginning of our first North Dakota winter clearing ice and snow by hand with shovels and picks, we decided to shop around for a snowblower. We had seen some neighbors make quick work of snow-packed driveways and sidewalks with their snowblowers. We found one, and it soon became *my* snowblower. I learned how to mix the gasoline and oil needed to fuel it and mastered the touchy choke. The sound of it sputtering to life was always something of a little win. Bundled up, I'd wrestle the machine across our driveway, feeling strong and capable, sometimes also clearing our neighbors' driveway too, just because I could.

Moms of young children often talk about how even mundane tasks like grocery shopping alone can become an escape, some "me time." Weirdly, clearing snow became that for me. Being outdoors in the freezing cold gave me time to clear my head and be completely alone. When I bundled up and announced I was going out to clear snow, the house became mysteriously quiet, the children suddenly studious and focused. Oh well, that worked for me. I watched the paths and driveway become bare under the mouth of the snowblower— even if only for a few brief hours before the next round of winter precipitation. I'd muse about decisions or challenges or even compose an article or outline in my head. Clearing snow gave me a lot of time for thinking. When Steve deployed to Iraq and was gone during the winter, I was thankful I knew how to handle the snowblower and the snow.

And it helped to remember the sunflowers would be back.

WHAT REALLY MATTERS

The long series of flights—from California, across the U.S., and over the ocean to Germany—was nearly over. During the last overnight flight from DC to Frankfurt, Steve and I had hoped to catch up on sleep we'd lost while traveling from the West Coast to the East Coast. But I shifted around uncomfortably the entire night, chasing a snooze without luck. Occasionally, I dozed off, only to be awakened by one of the four children whisper-shouting, "Mom!" in search of a snack or an answer to an obscure question or to climb over me to go to the restroom. A fitful night indeed.

After the long flight and waiting in line to clear customs, I stopped in the airport's restroom and surveyed myself in the mirror. Disheveled would be a generous description of my reflection: dark circles under my eyes and a rat's nest of hair. I looked like I had spent the last twenty-four hours traveling, finished off with a sleepless night strapped into an uncomfortable seat. Go figure. I did what I could to straighten myself up, running a brush ineffectively through my messy mop. In the three months before this move, I'd been through two major surgeries, a hysterectomy and a knee repair. My body was rebelling after hours spent in cramped conditions without rest. Sore, exhausted, and overwhelmed, I returned to one of the bathroom stalls, closed the toilet lid, sat down, and cried.

Aside from the physical exhaustion, I felt so *unqualified*. We were about to meet the general—who was Steve's new boss— his wife, Sue, and the welcoming party who'd be waiting for us at baggage claim. Steve had been hired to be Command Chief of one of the wings at Ramstein Air Base. While I was ever so proud and happy for him, I knew that a position like this one might come with certain unspoken expectations for the spouse—me. I could not imagine what the general and his wife would think of me. It wasn't just my current tired appearance featuring a wrinkled tee and jeans with apple juice spilled on them that worried me. I was a homeschooling mom who was most comfortable running around with my kids at the park, taxiing them to and from soccer practice, or immersing myself in a unit study on American history with my grade schoolers.

While Steve had been rising through the ranks over the previous years, I'd been content to be the one behind the scenes, taking care of the family, and playing a supportive role with little knowledge of the military world. I wasn't sure what expectations there would be for me as Steve stepped into this new role, nor how I would make it all work as a full-time homeschooling mom and continue to pursue my freelance writing career. In spite of my years of experience in military life, I felt unprepared for this new level of leadership and what it might require of me. Self-pity began to slip its unfriendly arms around me.

The overt expectation that military spouses should view their supportive roles as their full-time jobs officially ended years ago. However, the military continues to rely on the spouses of commanders, senior noncommissioned officers (NCOs), and other key personnel to facilitate family support. Many support programs for military families are fueled by volunteer spouses of all ranks and would simply not function without them. Much has been written and said about the unpaid effort military spouses provide and how much certain military programs rely on this effort. I absolutely agree that it's an issue that needs to be addressed, but many spouses— including me—could not leave that important work undone. It would feel like turning our backs on the needs of military families, a non-starter, especially during deployments. It's a sort of darned-if-you-do-darned-if-you-don't decision. All this went through my tired mind as I took on the weight of obligations and expectations yet unknown.

"Mom? Are you okay? Dad sent me to check on you," asked my twelve-year-old daughter Grace from the other side of the stall door. She sounded concerned.

"I'll be right out!" I called back with false cheerfulness. The children were already going through enough changes that come along with an overseas move. No need to add Mom-having-a-nervous-breakdown-in-a-foreign-airport to their list of worries.

I heard the outer door of the bathroom close as she left. I came out of the stall, sniffled, wiped my eyes, splashed some cold water on my face, and took a brave step out of the restroom. I had no idea what I'd be facing, but the only way through was forward.

The welcome group greeted us heartily and made us feel comfortable immediately. Of course, I should have remembered they would understand how tired we all were. They'd all made the same trek to Germany. They drove us to our new home on Ramstein Air Base, where an even warmer welcome awaited. Our kitchen counter was nearly covered with baskets of breakfast items, samples of wine, and yummy treats from nearby villages. Our pantry and fridge were stocked with water bottles and snacks. The goodies and gifts, along with kind welcome notes, were from the staff of Steve's new wing, the chief's group, and the other units on Ramstein. Our household goods were still in transit, of course, but Steve's new administrative assistant had arranged for our loaner furniture to be set up before we arrived. Even the beds were made and topped with thick comforters, ready for us to fall into. It was all so thoughtful and welcome after our long trip.

CHEER THEM ON

Over the next few days, we caught up on sleep, battled jetlag, and explored our new surroundings. Steve jumped right into his new position without a pause, while the kids and I transitioned into life in a new country, mostly on our own. Living in Germany was as picturesque—and foreign— as I'd imagined. The kids were excited about the novelty of everything from how to open the windows in our house to the way German street signs were different from American ones.

It was the end of winter, and we often wandered through the neighboring woods, searching for a peep of sun through the barren branches. We discovered a coffee shop right off base and spent many afternoons sampling tender, not-too-sweet cakes, flaky pastries, and steaming coffee. The kids and I had been taking German lessons before we'd arrived and now made our rudimentary attempts at speaking the language, often counting on our fingers slowly as we determined the number of whatever we were ordering—*eins, zwei, drei*—until inevitably the clerk or waiter would interrupt and let us know they spoke English. We did our best to speak in German and remember to say please—*bitte*—when ordering. The kids found a new favorite drink, a sparkling apple juice, or *Apfelschorle*. Little Anna could win even the sternest shopkeeper over by walking up to a counter and asking sweetly, "*Eine Apfelschorle, bitte?*"

Sue, the general's wife, was kind and helpful, checking in on us regularly to see how we were doing and if we needed anything. One day, she offered to pick me up and give me a tour of the base. As she told me her ideas and goals for supporting the wing's military spouses and families, she let me know I could help in whatever way I wanted, but there was no pressure for me to be involved. Talking about ways senior spouses can support military families, Sue said, "We're here to be their cheerleaders, their support," she said. "That's it."

That simple statement was one of the best pieces of advice I ever received as a seasoned military spouse. I noted the stark contrast between Sue's kind words and the very different behavior I'd observed from some other senior spouses, the *Do-you-know-who-my-husband-is?* type. I was so relieved, realizing that whatever effort I could offer would be welcome. We talked about the various spouse support groups, events for deployed families, the upcoming annual Air Force Ball, and meet-and-greets designed to help us get to know local community leaders.

Sadly, one of the first events we'd attend was a memorial service for a young airman who died, apparently by his own hand.

The year before our move to Germany had seen an enormous surge of U.S. troops deployed in Iraq and Afghanistan. No matter what service branch or career field your military member was in, it was likely they'd deploy at some point— or repeatedly. This was the reality for almost every military family. The constant deployment rotations to multiple war zones brought the inevitable fallout: casualties, combat stress and post-traumatic stress disorder, marital and family issues, and the rise of suicides.

At this first memorial service, I bowed my head in prayer and shed tears with everyone else over a life cut short. I felt a little uncomfortable about being seated at the front of the chapel alongside Steve, the general, and Sue. But Steve reminded me our visible presence was an important gesture of support for the grieving family and fellow airmen. I'll always remember the sight of that young man's mother. She stood in front of the altar to speak to those gathered to honor her son. Through her own unimaginable grief, she pleaded with her son's friends to remember that suicide is not the answer, that life is worth living. She asked them to remember how her son lived, not how he'd died. After the service, I simply squeezed her hand, at a loss for words.

Later, I reflected on the memorial service and remembered how I'd worried when we first arrived about my role and the expectations that came with Steve's new position. I had been so worried about being out of my element at formal events, concerned about military protocol and customs, wrapped up in my own feelings of inadequacy. Now, I knew the truth, and it was crystal clear: It really wasn't about me at all. Yes, formal events, military functions, and protocol would be part of our lives. As Steve's career progressed, we'd be treated with deference as VIPs; troops would snap to attention when he came into a room. But we'd also attend more funerals. Comfort more grieving families and friends. Sit in hard places that have no answers. Give our best efforts to support families of the deployed.

I realized there would be expectations for me and for Steve, but they were ones we wanted to fulfill: looking out for others, showing empathy, making sure military families had all the information and resources they needed. We'd be there for them. We'd do it because we'd been there once, too—a new military member, a scared young spouse, a family going through hardship alone while our servicemember was deployed.

I thought of my friend Sue's words to me, and I vowed I would never forget them:

"We're here to be their cheerleaders, their support. That's it."

THE FIRST BRAVE STEP

Rosetta's comfortably furnished apartment at Bob Hope Village exuded calm, a peaceful place to sit and appreciate the items gathered from her world travels. I would've guessed she was at least a decade younger than her seventy-nine years. My husband, Steve, and I were visiting her, and she showed us photos of her family from the 1960s, a slim young woman flanked by her handsome husband and three smiling children.

"He was a lucky guy!" Steve commented.

"No," Rosetta responded quietly, "I was the lucky one."

She met her Air Force husband at Eglin Air Force Base and married him in 1956. His name was Al, but Rosetta said she rarely called him anything but "Honey."

For a small-town girl from Mississippi, a new life as an Air Force wife seemed like something out of a movie, an adventure. And Rosetta was ready to take the first brave step.

"Everything was new and exciting, and I couldn't wait to see what would come next," she said. "We never questioned orders. When the military says to go, you go!"

The couple's first move was to Alaska, and they made the final leg of their journey on a Navy ship, setting off from Seattle. Rosetta and Al lived in Anchorage for three years, stationed at Elmendorf Air Force Base. Rosetta said Alaska stole her heart right away, and when Al's final military assignment took them back to Elmendorf, they were thrilled to revisit the place they'd adored so much as a young couple. She loved watching the moon peek over the mountains, soaking in the spectacular sight of the northern lights, and adventuring during trips in their little camper.

"It's so beautiful that it's hard to describe," she said. "Once you live there, it really becomes 'my Alaska'."

Military life would end up planting Al and Rosetta's growing family in locations like Turkey, Washington, DC, and

North Carolina. Their children modeled their parents' attitude of embracing each experience.

"One of the most meaningful trips we took was to the Holy Land when we were stationed in Turkey. We took our children along with us in a group with a seven-car caravan. It was so crazy that we were even able to get in and out, as the Six-Day War happened shortly after we left. At the time, we just knew it was a once-in-a-lifetime experience. We saw all the places you read about in the Bible, the cedars of Lebanon, Jordan, Damascus . . ."

Rosetta credited her mother for teaching her to be open to new experiences and to new people.

"My mother always modeled being kind to everyone," she said. "The richness of the melting pot of the military and all the friendships I made were so intriguing. I just loved it."

That attitude of embracing whatever life sent her way would serve her well in the coming years, even long after their Air Force days. After Al's retirement in the 1970s, the couple moved to Pennsylvania where they lived for many years until Al's death. Some years after Al died, Rosetta realized it was time for her to move again, even though she'd been in Pennsylvania for forty years by that time.

"I was sitting there alone in a big house, and thought, *This is too much, just for me.* Sometimes the kids would visit, but days, weeks, and even a month would pass by, and I thought, *All right, it's time for me to just go do my own thing.*"

Rosetta heard about Bob Hope Village and traveled with her sisters to tour the area. Jets from nearby Eglin AFB flew overhead, and when she heard the familiar sound, she knew she was home.

The move brought her full circle, back to the base where Al was stationed when they first met and fell in love. I asked if moving to Florida was difficult, if she grieved her old life after living so long in Pennsylvania.

"I felt like God wanted me to come here, like he directed all the details," she said. "I've always felt God's hand since I was a little girl, no matter the circumstances. I've always had this peace that wherever I am is where I'm supposed to be. I truly do believe in divine providence."

Still, she said she will always miss Al—Honey—after their forty-four years of marriage. She said she could still hear him singing to her like he used to when he'd walk into a room: *"Have I told you lately that I love you?"*

Even after his death, she said she continued to find love notes he had written to her or poems he'd printed out and hidden in her cookbooks. Their love truly did span a lifetime.

"He was an amazing father and grandfather," said Rosetta. "He worked, then coached the kids' sports teams in the evenings and was such an involved dad. He was my life."

Embracing change and adventure may look like leaping into new experiences across the globe, while helping your children feel safe and secure, like Rosetta did for years. It might also be taking control of your life after loss and moving forward on your own terms.

No matter how old you are, there's still a big world out there, with much to offer, if you're willing to take the first brave step.

PART 3

DIFFICULT STORIES

FINDING STRENGTH AND HOPE

Courage doesn't always roar. Sometimes courage is the quiet voice at the end of the day saying, "I will try again tomorrow."
– Mary Anne Radmacher

I'm not certain I would have called myself a "military spouse" in the early years of my marriage. Yes, the military dictated where we lived, as I learned with my first military move to Wright-Patterson AFB. But as far as I was concerned, the Air Force was just Steve's employer. He was in a career field that didn't deploy often, if at all, in the early 1990s. He'd come into the military as a computer programmer, worked in the Communications, or COMM Squadron, and enjoyed a fairly routine work week. The military was his job. It came with occasional social obligations, awards dinners, and ceremonies, but it didn't define our family life. Not yet. And I had no idea how much the changes and challenges of the coming years would change and challenge us all.

One crisp fall morning in Ohio, I sat my toddler in his highchair to watch *Sesame Street* and sprinkled a few Cheerios across his tray to keep him occupied. I checked on the baby—lulled to sleep by the rocking of his baby swing—and then I stepped out on the porch to get the morning paper. I was hoping to sit down for a few quiet moments and catch up on news in the world outside my little bubble, which featured lots of spitting up and diaper changes just then.

As I stepped back into the warm house, I glanced down at the paper in my hand. The front-page headlines screamed the news of an unknown number of American service members killed during a military operation in Mogadishu, Somalia. But what made me drop the paper was the graphic photo of dead American soldiers being dragged through the streets by a jeering crowd.[1] It was a horrifying image; one I'll never forget. These were young men, many of them the same age and rank as my own husband. I could only imagine what their families were feeling. I sat down and cried for them, for their families, and for their futures cut short.

Until that morning, I hadn't thought much about the oath Steve had taken when he joined the military and vowed to serve our country. The truth that it meant everything—even his life if required—began to settle into my soul that day.

Some years later, after several moves across the country and two more children added to our family, the world was shocked by the events of 9/11, which changed the nation and the trajectory of the lives of military families.

DEFINING MOMENTS

After the attacks of September 11, 2001, we walked through the horror and grief with the rest of the country. We were living in base housing at MacDill AFB, Florida, at the time and we saw our normal life come to an abrupt halt. All U.S. military installations were put on Force Protection Condition Delta, the highest level of force protection. The military made it clear that no one would be driving on base without a darn good reason, like going to work or coming back home to base housing. Everything that went through the gates of the base had to be cleared. Armed security forces inspected each vehicle with bomb-sniffing dogs and used mirrors on long poles to check vehicle undercarriages for explosives.

Previously mundane errands of daily life, such as dropping kids off at soccer practice, now required waiting in a long line of cars and commercial trucks at the gate. The incongruous sight of snipers on the commissary rooftop were jarring the first time but became a surreal norm after a while. Steve was assigned to U.S. Central Command, or CENTCOM, which ran all the operations in Southwest Asia. After 9/11, long work hours, sleeping at his office, and repeated deployments became the norm, as it did for military members worldwide.

With the deployments and the inevitable stress and fear that came along for the ride, I understood I could no longer distance myself from other military spouses or the support we'd need to get through the coming years. Going it alone was simply not an option. Pretending that life was normal was impossible, as we went about everyday tasks like running errands and taking kids to the library or the park. Impossible and even ridiculous with the backdrop of absent spouses and heightened security on the base. It affected everything and everyone we knew. What we didn't know then was how long the war would go on—or how the rhythm of deployment and security issues would become ingrained in our lives.

I'd never been the type to get deeply involved in spouse clubs or events, though I'd been to a few gatherings. It wasn't that I had anything against them, but we'd naturally connected with friends and community through church or activities and sports with our kids.

During Steve's first deployment to Iraq, that all changed. By this time, we'd moved to Grand Forks AFB in North Dakota, and about one-third of his unit deployed to Baghdad. With four young children, I had no experience navigating as a solo parent through a deployment—not yet. It was new to most of us, and it was also the first Iraq deployment for Steve's squadron commander. He and his wife Kathy had four small children, too. Right away, Kathy and I recognized our mutual needs and responsibilities and decided to join forces.

There was no formal support program for spouses at the time, so Kathy and I developed a plan to support the deployed families in the squadron and to also look out for each other. We planned weekly check-in calls to all the spouses, helped with issues like coordinating childcare, set up regular in-person deployment support meetings and fun events. We fielded calls about lost military IDs and other questions, kept contact with the unit's first sergeant about any issues or resources needed, and we acted as a sounding board for worried spouses. Some hard things happened during those months, and communication with our husbands was limited because of their location. Kathy and I took turns being on call for the other spouses, so we would each have time off when we didn't have to take calls at all hours. During my spouse check-in calls, I added Kathy to my list and called to ask how she was doing, and she did the same for me. This simple plan helped us both get through that time.

Many years and more separations and deployments later, I began to notice how much military life defined me. How could it not? I not only identified as a military spouse, but I also embraced that identity. I began to appreciate the instant camaraderie and shared experiences with other military families.

It is important to have our own identity, to pursue our dreams and passions as individuals, but it does no good to pretend that military life doesn't affect who we are and who we will become. It will, whether we accept that truth or not. The military has a say in where we live, when our children change schools, and how often or little we see our spouses. Military service has also impacted so many families with injuries, illness, post-traumatic stress, even death. It isn't just another job, a role our spouses can take off and put away when they come home from work. It's a way of life with an influence that is all-encompassing.

For that reason, finding support and community with other military spouses made the difference for me. That young woman who could barely open her mouth to speak to strangers learned that reaching out and forging bonds with others was what would get her through both the difficult times and the good times. I am certain I could not have walked through those dark, uncertain days of deployment without the community and support of other military spouses. I know the many moves and transitions our family has been through have been better because of the military community that surrounds us.

Because of what we've been through together, I'm proud to be in that community. I'm proud to call myself a military spouse.

THE DEPLOYMENT ACHE

> i carry your heart with me (i carry it in
> my heart) i am never without it (anywhere
> i go you go, my dear; and whatever is done
> by only me is your doing, my darling)
> —e.e. cummings

Steve was scheduled to leave for Iraq a couple of days after Christmas, and the overarching feeling I remember from that holiday season was a constant sense of dread. Everything was colored by it, that apprehension, as if someone had taken a broad brush and painted over my entire life with a washed out gray. I moved around in a fog. Since that first deployment, our military family has experienced more and more deployments and separations. Younger military spouses often ask me, "Do deployments get easier?"

My answer to that is yes and no.

Yes, it does get easier because you know what to expect; and, no, it's not easier at all because, well, you know what to expect.

Your mind and heart are elsewhere, but somehow you must carry on with the normality of life: commuting to work, picking up groceries, running kids to school and soccer and dance and playdates. All while your thoughts scream, *I haven't heard from my loved one in thirty-six hours! Is he okay? Am I going to see his face on the news?*

If military life is like a rollercoaster with its ups and downs, military deployment is the mother of all rollercoasters with corkscrew turns, terrifying climbs, and upside-down plunges. Like many long-term military spouses, I've cultivated what might be considered an inappropriately grim sense of humor over the years that became something of a shield for me. It has seen me through weird and hard times, but there are moments that even I can't laugh my way through.

As a child, I suffered from frequent bouts of insomnia. I remember creeping back down the hallway after I'd been tucked into bed. I'd crouch around the corner from the living room, listening to the end of the ten o'clock news until I heard the closing theme music. When the creak of the recliner signaled that my dad was getting up to head for bed, I'd scuttle back to my room.

There I would lie awake, clutching the covers under my chin, my body tense, heart racing, listening for the clicks of the light switches throughout the house, knowing the darkness was coming and I was helpless to stop it. I'd stare at the ceiling, long after everyone else was asleep, unable to still my thoughts, no matter how I tried to convince myself.

Just relax. Go to sleep. You have to get up early for school.

No amount of talking to myself could help when my old friend insomnia paid a visit.

An impending deployment stirred up those same childhood feelings at bedtime, making it hard for me to sleep. I was plagued by dread, helplessness, and useless self-talk.

I recently came across some journal entries and private blog posts I wrote for our family during Steve's deployments over the course of a decade. Reading them again reminds me of how confused my heart often felt—and how raw.

I remember the day I wrote this entry. Our youngest was about six years old at the time.

We said goodbye to Steve yesterday as he left for another deployment, knowing that the next time we see him, birthdays, Thanksgiving, and Christmas will have passed without him. Beyond the big events, we'll have missed the little things together—laughter, conversation, family time, shared memories. Part of me wonders . . . How can we keep doing this? I won't lie—it's so very, very difficult.

In my soul, I feel like I'm somehow both drowning and parched at the same time.

One of the hardest deployments we dealt with was when Steve was given only a couple of weeks' notice that he was going to Afghanistan—*for a year.* We were stationed in Germany and needed to quickly decide what I and our four kids would do. Should we move back to the States to be near family or stay put? We concluded that staying overseas made sense. Our two oldest were in high school, involved in activities and our base chapel's youth group. The kids all had a strong support system that would be difficult to replicate, and we knew we'd have to move again when Steve returned, as he was due for a new assignment after this deployment. Here's a private blog entry from that time.

Without going into too much detail, we found out that Steve will be leaving for a year-long deployment very soon. We are already stationed overseas, and to say we're stunned is an understatement. Still, as I look back at the weeks leading up to this latest, I see God's hand through it all and His tender care. More than I can ever share here. One little thing I can say is that a year ago, this news would have been devastating to me physically, since I was still recovering from surgery. I'm in a much better place now, and for that I'm grateful.

It's best if I don't ever assume I know what's "best" because I rarely do. The next year will look much different than I had expected. There are some things I'll need to do to make it while he's gone (we've been down this road before): more naps, more patience, more flexibility. Also, probably more fast food and TV watching! Knowing that there are going to be many tearful days and sleepless nights for all of us.

One little detail I always seemed to forget about deployment: the exhaustion. It's taxing to deal with all your kids' needs and their fears—plus your own. (Hats off to single parents everywhere, by the way.) Maybe this forgetfulness about deployment is similar to post-childbirth amnesia that makes you think that having another child won't be such a big deal. Here's one mid-deployment journal entry, when that feeling that there's no end in sight leaves me feeling like a wrung-out dishcloth.

> We are just kind of moving along, coping with Steve's latest deployment, spending time with each other and friends, doing church activities, homeschooling, and going to soccer practices, piano lessons, and Awanas, and all those other things that are part of life with kids and a lonely mommy taxiing them around. I'm a bit tired of that last part. Frankly, I'm just tired.

> I read recently that having a loved one deployed is akin to dealing with a severe long-term illness or family trauma. It's an incredible stress. One thing I notice is that, over time, most other people become accustomed to the situation and quit asking me how I'm doing. It's just the way it is.

> I think with any ongoing stress or difficulty, people react and respond appropriately in the beginning, and then life goes on.

> For them.

And from another deployment:
> It's also been almost six months since Steve left for his latest deployment . . . which means we are at the half-way point, which means . . . we still have (gulp) six months left. I'm really trying to view this milestone as a positive thing, rather than the fact that I have as much time in front of me as what we've just been through. In the interest of not being too depressing, I won't go on and on about the difficulties. Things

DO seem magnified when he's gone, that much I'll admit. Little difficulties and big trials, of which we've had both.

I also just plain miss him.

WOULD YOU GO WITH ME?

Several years before his last deployment, Steve and I heard the song "Would You Go with Me?" by Josh Turner. We looked at each other and said, "This is our song!" The lyrics seemed to express so well what we'd already been through in our married life, the promises we'd made. Yes, I would go with him. I did leave it all behind, even though I didn't understand what that meant when I made that promise. During that last deployment, I seemed to hear the song everywhere I went: in line at the grocery store, on the radio in the minivan, even on TV.

"Would you go with me?" it asked me again and again, coming at me when I least expected it.

Yes, even though it hurts so much, but I'm so tired of being alone.

When I'm around other families going through deployment, I hope I'll always remember how smothering and all-encompassing the aloneness could feel. I penned these lines one lonely morning:

Don't forget about us.

Deployments don't get easier, no matter how many times we've been through it or how capable we may seem.

I always get a bit contemplative as the end of a deployment nears. During one tough deployment season, we lost two active-duty friends, I'd been through a major illness that set me back a couple of months, and another dear friend was diagnosed with cancer. Life seemed to lurch from one hardship to another, and I grappled to find the meaning in it all. My journal during that time reflected my struggle to identify a purpose in the pain:

I was telling a friend recently that I wasn't really sure what exactly the lesson was that I was supposed to "get" over this past year. There had to be something. Surely God was trying to teach me something. I don't believe hardship is ever wasted. At that moment, I couldn't understand any of it. She has recently come through cancer treatments herself and remarked, "Maybe there is no lesson. Maybe it was just about holding on." It may sound simple, but I do believe it's also this: treasure every moment. There is never a guarantee of another single day. Live each day the best you can and squeeze all the life out of it that you can get. Don't take your loved ones for granted. Love them. Thank God for all the blessings, big and small.

When I look back over this year, I know it was a time of stretching . . . painful growth in many ways, unexpected ways. But there were also unexpected blessings . . . sometimes the people you think will be there for you aren't the ones who are. But on the flip side, others come out of the woodwork to lend a hand and or say a kind word. As the saying goes, "There is no desolation without some consolation."

I realized during those wearisome deployment days that willing myself to "be okay with it" never worked, like my childish attempts to will away my insomnia. Sleep eventually came to me—and so would the end of a deployment. But until it did, I had to keep moving forward through the dark days, the hopeful days, the endless days, and the days when I didn't feel like I could go on.

Maybe you feel this way, too, whether it's over deployment or another challenge. I memorized a poem during middle school that has comforted me over the years. It reminds me that the sun will shine again. It must. And so will my heart.

The day is cold, and dark, and dreary;
It rains, and the wind is never weary;
The vine still clings to the mouldering wall,
But at every gust the dead leaves fall,
And the day is dark and dreary.

My life is cold, and dark, and dreary;
It rains, and the wind is never weary;
My thoughts still cling to the mouldering Past,
But the hopes of youth fall thick in the blast,
And the days are dark and dreary.
Be still, sad heart! and cease repining;
Behind the clouds is the sun still shining;
Thy fate is the common fate of all,
Into each life some rain must fall,
Some days must be dark and dreary.
(Henry Wadsworth Longfellow, "The Rainy Day")

THE YEAR I WATCHED *GILMORE GIRLS*

While talking with a young military spouse friend, she lamented over how little she'd accomplished during the year her husband was deployed.

"I just feel like I didn't meet any of the goals I set for myself while he was gone," she said as we sipped our skinny mocha-somethings at the Starbucks on base.

"I didn't run that marathon. I didn't finish losing the weight I wanted—"

"Wait a second," I stopped her.

"You took several college classes. You homeschooled your girls!" I gestured at those sweet girls, dressed in matching outfits, blissfully slurping hot chocolate at the table beside us.

"You didn't just keep your girls alive—you *thrived*! Look how happy they are!"

I am not one to pretend things are great when they are not, so she knew I wasn't blowing smoke. And this conversation reminded me of that one year. The year I watched the *Gilmore Girls*.

Now, just in case you think I'm going to go on about how I sat on the couch an entire year, let me reassure you—*I am*.

Yes. In this era of social media, boss babe influencers, hustle culture, and vision boards dedicated to productivity, it almost seems sacrilegious to encourage other military spouses to (gasp!) do nothing. But I am going to do just that. I hope that you will take some time once in a while to *do nothing*.

Hear me out. As I've mentioned, during Steve's last deployment we were stationed in Germany. Our four teens and I opted to stay there while he was gone, because we felt settled and surrounded by a strong community. The kids were plugged in with school, dance, and sports, and we were grateful for the fact that they'd have mentors in their lives while their dad was gone for so long. Through the fall, we cruised along, and I got pretty smug about how we were doing.

We've got this. We're pros at this whole deployment thing.

And then winter hit. The dismal, gray German winter that lasts for months and months and months. Yes, Germany is beautiful, but the long bleak months of winter coupled with typical deployment woes wreaked havoc with my mental health. Suddenly, it seemed time was crawling. The deployment felt endless. One blustery Friday, as I was running errands, I stopped by the video rental store on base (remember those?) to pick out something to watch on our regular movie and popcorn night. I came across an orange DVD case that set me on an unexpected journey. It was *Gilmore Girls*.

Gilmore Girls. I'd heard of it, obviously. It was the chick-flick kind of TV show that my husband would not willingly watch. So why not give it a try while he was gone? And with that, my fate was sealed for the next 153 episodes.

I immediately fell in love with Lorelai's fast-talking, wise-cracking ways. The relationship between her and daughter Rory warmed my heart. I loved the town of Stars Hollow where they lived. I wanted to live in Stars Hollow. Lorelai's icy relationship with her mother Emily reminded me of some (*cough, cough*) challenging extended family relationships of my own.

I reached the end of the first DVD and knew I was hooked. Conveniently, the video store was on the way to my oldest son's baseball practices, so he agreed to return the first DVD and pick up my next installment. And the next and the next. Sweet boy!

During that year, I set many goals: sewing a quilt, learning to love running, and cleaning out my craft and linen closets. I didn't meet all of them, but I *did* continue to work on my free-lance writing career, transported kids to dance and sports and church, homeschooled them all, and did volunteer work on base. We took weekend sightseeing trips to nearby countries like Switzerland, Belgium, France, and the Netherlands. However, a long bout with bronchitis set back my attempts at running. The week in which all of our car batteries died seemed like an extreme manifestation of Murphy's Law. A series of weird encounters with troublesome neighbors added to my sense of isolation.

With all of that, in mid-winter, in the thick of the seemingly constant overcast weather, recurring insomnia, worrying over and missing Steve, I thought of a new objective: I could finish every *Gilmore Girls* episode before deployment's end. Now *this* was a doable goal. My daughters sometimes joined me. While I yelled at Rory to hang on to Dean, they were firmly Team Jess. The characters drew me and kept me company. What could Lorelai possibly see in irresponsible, drifty Christopher? Would she and Luke *finally* get together? And who wouldn't want a supportive, funny best friend like Sookie?

During the holidays, the kids and I traveled back to the States to visit family, and I took a break from Lorelai, Rory and Co. for a time. However, I resumed my regimen on return. I am nothing if not disciplined. Those late-night hours I might have spent staring at the ceiling, trying to sleep or worrying over the latest news about Steve's location weren't wasted—I had to find out whether or not Paris and Rory were accepted to Harvard!

By the time Rory left for college and took up with that cad Logan—I never did trust his eyes—it was beginning to look a bit like springtime in Germany. It was also around this time that my son informed me he was resigning from his position as DVD courier, as the video store employees had taken to calling him "The Gilmore Guy."

Gilmore Girl watching hit a bit of a bump when Steve received orders for his next assignment before he returned home from the desert. It was up to me to take on the mountain of tasks that go along with an overseas move. And then redo the whole thing when the Air Force changed our assignment—after the moving trucks were already loaded and on their way. I ended up at the base transportation office in tears, holding new sets of orders and my trusty power of attorney, pleading, "Help, please."

Still, duplicate tasks and paperwork notwithstanding, I had only twenty episodes of *Gilmore Girls* left. I'd made it this far. *Could I see it through?* I realized that I could. I may not have run a marathon, but I would make it through all seven seasons, by golly.

Several days before my husband came home, I clicked "eject" and put the last DVD in its case to return to the store. I'd done it! I hadn't sewn that quilt, logged as many running miles as I'd hoped, nor discovered the bottom of my craft closet, but I had seen *Gilmore Girls* through to the end. Psychologist types would probably say the draw of this show was the reminder of home, comfort, and normality, and there's probably some truth to that. No matter, my time with Lorelai and Rory was *my time*. And that's okay.

The military spouses I've known through the years are extremely productive people. They are small business owners, professionals, volunteers, moms, and friends. They're the quintessential multi-taskers. They're the team parents, soccer coaches, and first on your list of emergency contacts. Many are all these things and also hold down the fort alone while their spouse is away for deployment or training. I honestly don't know one who should be doing more. (And if you do have extra time, please let me know. I have a few closets that need organizing.)

Many of us Type A, goal-oriented folks don't believe down time is productive. We think we always need to be *doing* something. We hustle. We grind. We revel in being busy. Down time feels—well—unproductive. But sometimes—trust me on this—a little downtime is just what you need. Taking a break is what helps you to stay productive. It's not lazy. So, take this as permission to relax a moment, sit a spell, and just be. As my grandmother would wisely repeat, "You're a human *being*, not a human *doing*."

And I'm not going to tell you if Luke and Lorelai made it work. You'll have to take some downtime to watch for yourself!

TWENTY YEARS OF WAR

I sailed past the protestors outside the base gate in my red mini-van, honking repeatedly as I stuck my hand out the window, flipping the bird. My middle school son was old enough to realize what I was doing and gasped from the middle seat, "Mom! I'm telling Dad!"

"Go ahead," I replied grimly. "I'm so tired of this."

It was early in the Iraq War, and military families were facing weeks and months of deployment—which would add up to years spent apart. While families grappled with these facts and many unknowns—protesters of the Iraq War decided a good place to display their opposition was right outside the gates of MacDill AFB, Florida, where we lived. On any typical weekday afternoon, minivans and SUVs filled with military families were lined up to clear security and return home to military housing after music lessons, sports practices, or school.

"YOU'RE KILLERS," the signs screamed in bold letters, or "THEIR BLOOD IS ON YOUR HANDS," sometimes along with graphic photos. I did my best to shield or distract my children from the worst of the disturbing signs, but everyone has their breaking point. Mine was my eight-year-old son's response to the signs.

"Are we really killers?" he squeaked out on our way home from the library one afternoon. That's when I snapped and threw my hand out the window in a one-finger salute. I'm certain it did no good, other than to allow me to vent. But in my opinion, the location of the protest did no good either. The anti-war crowd's beef was not with us, well, it shouldn't have been. To my mind, it was akin to berating a barista for a decision handed down by Starbucks headquarters. Military members, and *especially* the families left behind, did not have anything to do with policy decisions. During what was already a stressful and difficult time, the presence of these protestors only added more.

My husband served thirty-one years in the world's greatest Air Force. I've told him he's *legendary* because the Air Force is our nation's youngest service branch, and by the time he'd retired, he'd been around for nearly half its history. We're a proud military family, and our son also served on active duty and went on two deployments.

I'd been a military spouse for thirteen years when 9/11 happened and changed everything, not just for our country and the world, but for our military families. Of course, like anyone else who lived through it, I will never ever forget that day. And in the aftermath, deployment suddenly became an everyday word, not just for certain career fields in the military, but for everyone. Most military members would now take their turn deploying, many multiple times.

Steve deployed several times, including time spent in both Iraq and Afghanistan. All told, we spent *years* apart due to deployments, like so many other military families.

Our four young children lived through those years, too. I'll never forget our twelve-year-old son's reaction to his dad leaving for Baghdad. After we'd dropped Steve off to catch the military transport plane, I found our son huddled in his closet crying. He was hiding because he was worried it would upset me if I knew he was upset.

All of our children struggled with these separations, missing their dad and knowing he could be in danger. Sometimes it was more than their young minds could take in.

"I want him h-h-home—*right*—now!" My youngest daughter threw herself face down on her bed, each word of her cry punctuated with a frustrated sob. Then five years old, she simply didn't have the capacity to understand why her dad couldn't tuck her into bed—*again*.

Though we'd explained to her where Steve was and how long he'd be gone, she was *done with it*. Frankly, so was I. Her clenched fists and tear-streaked face mirrored my own feelings, and I would have thrown a tantrum right along with her if I thought it would bring him home.

Steve's final long deployment happened while our older two were in high school. We gave up time with him, we gave up the ability to make memories with him, we gave up normal life. Steve missed everything during our oldest son Matthew's senior year, as he was gone from July of one year to July of the next: award ceremonies, prom, baseball games, college visits, and applications. He missed our other son Gabriel's high school drumline debut, his first missions trip with his youth group, our girls' dance recitals and soccer games, normal family moments, regular squabbles over chores, and many holidays and birthdays. Our family will never get that time back.

And yet, I'm fully aware that others gave up so much more. They gave up limbs. They gave up their physical health, mental health, their marriages. *Some gave their lives.* These are debts our country can never repay.

For the most part, the politics of the wars were completely immaterial to our family's experience in the moment. A deployment, whether to Iraq, Afghanistan, or anywhere else, was a challenge we had to face as a military family. That's what made me so angry at the anti-war protesters shouting at us—military spouses and children—who were just trying to get home and deal with life while our loved ones were far away putting their lives on the line.

The end of the Afghanistan war in 2021 brought painful feelings to the surface again. Most Americans seemed to agree that it was time to be done in Afghanistan after twenty years, though the majority of our country barely noticed we were at war during much of that time. Many military people also agreed it was time to bring the conflict to an end, but those who fought that war deserved a better ending to those decades of sacrifice—as did the people of Afghanistan and our allies.

After the abrupt withdrawal of the U.S. from Afghanistan—during which thirteen service members lost their lives—I heard from a lot of military spouses. A common theme was, *We're angry.* They were upset by the loss of life, and they also feared their family's sacrifices through all the years of war in Afghanistan were meaningless. They'd endured years of deployment, followed by medical issues, post-traumatic stress, and problems reintegrating after deployment as a family; and they felt betrayed by their own country. The truth is: If your family has been marked by years of Middle East and other deployments, you're not alone; and your sacrifices and service will never be nullified.

"My ex-husband was never the same," said a woman who asked to remain anonymous. "Each deployment to Afghanistan made it worse. The shame and anger of PTSD held him tightly and pushed us apart after the third deployment. The sad thing is that I never stopped loving the person that he was before deployment, and he never found that person again. We ended things and I always wonder, *What if a piece of him hadn't died out there?*"

Whatever your military family is facing—deployments past, present, or future—find healthy ways to cope and make mental and physical health a priority. When you can't control what's going on around you, it's important to step back and take care of yourself, whatever that looks like: time alone, staying active, starting a project, reaching out, or connecting with other military or veteran spouses. Take a look at the list of resources and supportive agencies at the end of this book if you need help to process all that has happened. We may not be able to solve all the world's problems or affect policy, but we *can* make our own health and our military family's health a priority.

In the meantime, please take care of yourself. *You're important. We need you.*

And wherever you have served this country, please know that your service will never, ever be forgotten. We owe you everything.

LESSONS FROM A CEMETERY

Over ten thousand service members dead. 10,481, to be exact.

As I gazed across endless fields dotted with precise rows of grave markers, I choked back a sob. Steve looked at me, curious. It wasn't as if I knew any of the dead or was related in some way. But still. Each grave signified someone's husband, son, brother, grandchild, uncle, cousin, or friend.

I could barely take in this visual reminder of the loss of life. We were attending Memorial Day ceremonies at the Lorraine American Cemetery in St. Avold, France, where the largest number of American service members killed in Europe during World War II have been laid to rest.[2] My husband and other military members from Ramstein Air Base in Germany had been asked to represent the current-day American military.

Under looming gray skies that threatened rain, Steve and I arrived late after taking several wrong turns on our drive through the picturesque French countryside and villages. Now we attempted to get ourselves in hand before we were seated with the official party— he straightened the jacket of his service dress, replete with ribbons and awards earned over two decades of an Air Force career, and I fumbled to pry open a stubborn umbrella over my suit jacket and freshly sprayed hair.

The day hadn't been a smooth one so far. It had taken me the better part of the morning to hunt through my collection of mom-wear for appropriate clothing for an outdoor spring ceremony, settling on a rarely worn matching suit jacket and skirt. When I realized my only pair of hose had a rip in them, I'd switched to pants, which put us behind schedule to get there at noon. It was an eighty-kilometer drive from one country to the next, and we'd gotten a little lost following the penciled directions to the cemetery.

Worried about being late for a commemoration put on by our allies and neighbors, we approached the cemetery nestled beside the sleepy French town of St. Avold and swung into an empty spot in the packed parking lot. Breathless, we strode up the hill to where we could see the crowd gathering. We moved as quickly as people can when they're in military service dress (him) and not-often-worn high heels (me).

The thought crossed my mind that it seemed a bit humid to be outdoors in this type of attire, and I was already looking forward to Memorial Day plans later that day that didn't involve dressing up. We hurried around the corner of a low stone wall and came face to face with rolling hills that flanked fields upon fields of our countrymen slumbering beneath the bright green sod.

Thoughts of messed up hairdos, arriving late, even future plans fell away. We both stopped to survey the scene for a moment, the need for hurry forgotten. On each grave fluttered two small flags, one American and one French, placed there earlier in the day by schoolchildren. As we were seated for the ceremony, I couldn't take my eyes off the white rows of marble crosses and Stars of David that marked each resting place. Each one was *someone*, not a number. As a military spouse, one of my greatest nightmares was the thought of losing my own husband to war. And here the earth offered up a stark reminder of what had happened so many years before, pleading that we would not forget this loss.

Etched on the chapel wall at the Lorraine Cemetery are words from Dwight D. Eisenhower:

> *Here we and all who shall hereafter live in freedom will be reminded that to these men and their comrades we owe a debt to be paid with grateful remembrance of their sacrifice and with high resolve that the cause for which they died shall live.*

The cause for which they died shall live.

To those whose family members lie under the ground in Lorraine, I'm certain these words are full of meaning. To the other hundreds of thousands of families who received a knock at the door, a call, or a telegram with the worst news possible, that their loved one is the latest casualty, it means everything.

To those of us left behind is assigned the task of remembering. To not let their sacrifice be forgotten. To resolve to live in freedom.

But what does that look like? We all know that none of us is guaranteed another tomorrow. Yet, those somber reminders tend to get pushed to the back of my mind when faced with normal life again.

After that day at the Lorraine Cemetery, I of course went back to my regular life and got too quickly caught up in daily checklists, meetings, and the hundreds of little worries and tasks that make up any day.

But every so often, I still stop and remember. I remember the sacrifice. Remember what they gave. Remember their families, who had to learn to carry on without the ones they loved.

THE KIDS WILL BE OKAY, RIGHT?

My husband had served on active duty for over twenty-five years when our oldest son announced that he'd decided to join the military, too. It came as a bit of a shock to us, as Matt had always discussed other career plans before that time.

I wrote in a column in *Military Spouse* magazine about the conflicting feelings that assailed me when our son left for basic training and how different it was to watch my own child take on a life of service as opposed to my husband, whom I'd always known as a military member. Steve had always been an airman to me. Now, I understood what his own mother must have felt when Steve joined the military. I poured out my heart in that column, writing in part:

I remember you . . . grabbing your Daddy's BDU shirt he'd casually tossed on the couch after work. You wrapped it around your adorable toddler self and pattered around the living room, the hem of the shirt dragging on the ground behind you, the sleeves so long they tripped you.

You were still little enough to have dimples in your elbows. I remember the morning you crammed your Barney backpack full of crayons, coloring books, and Matchbox cars so you could go to work with Daddy. I still have the photo of you both posing by the door before you left. He, tall and handsome in his blues; you, standing on tiptoe to reach up for his big hand.

I never imagined you'd go into the military, too.

It is different with you, of course, and I feel fiercely protective. . . . I was not prepared for the wave of emotion that threatened to choke me the day you boarded the plane to leave for basic training. I've always had the mindset of the all-volunteer force, you know: "If no one volunteers, where will our country be?"

But I will admit that there are times when dark thoughts hit me in the quiet hours of the night: "The military has my husband–does it need my child, too? With all the policy changes lately, is this a good decision for you and your wife? What about my future grandchildren? Will the military be good to you all? Is it worthy of you?"

Whether or not your military child takes on military service, there's a certain amount of grief that comes along for the ride when our kids grow up. Our family was a tight-knit group, traveling the world together and often only having each other to lean on in a new location. Of course, as we logged the years, I spent time worrying how the pressures and changes of military life would affect our children as grown-ups, since I'd had no experience with it myself.

Author Pat Conroy, son of a career Marine, said, "We spent our entire childhoods in the service of our country, and no one even knew we were there."[3]

But I knew. And I recognized the unique sacrifices and challenges our children, all military children, were making.

One day when we were living in Germany, I was flipping through the TV channels and landed on American Forces Network, which was re-airing a documentary called *Brats: Our Journey Home*, about the lives of military children of the twentieth century. (I know many of us don't care for the term "military brat," but for good or bad, it stuck and is the origin of the title of this film.) As I watched, I sat down on the coffee table and reeled a bit as now-adult military brats vented about their growing up years and the issues they'd battled later in life. Some of the common problems included feelings of rootlessness, struggles maintaining long-term relationships, and even substance abuse. I was overwhelmed to think that this could be the outcome for our four children. The voices on the television made it seem inevitable.

Just then, thirteen-year-old Grace walked in and noticed me sitting in stunned silence, tears rolling down my cheeks. She listened while I babbled on about how sorry I was that they had to move so much—that their dad was deployed again—that I was just *so, so sorry* about all of it. Her older siblings joined us.

"Mom, it's okay. Really."

I blinked back the tears and regarded my children as they assured me. They wanted me to know they were okay. Yes, there were hurdles involved in this military lifestyle, but my kids, all in middle school and high school at that point, rushed to assure me that they wouldn't trade their lives for anything.

During this time, I often wrote about resources for military children and the need for parents to be aware of our kids' struggles and how we could find help to support them. I was speaking to myself as much as anyone else. As online keyboard warriors tend to do, several came out of the woodwork to admonish me for worrying.

"The kids will be just fine," said some. "If you don't make a big deal out of it, they won't either," said others.

Um, okay—but it *is* difficult to pull up stakes and move across the world, no matter your age. It *isn't* normal to regularly have a parent away for months or years at a time, often in an unsafe location, not to mention a place where others actively wish to do them harm. I can't even imagine the fears they dealt with over those years. No amount of glib, happy talk or positivity can wipe away what they endured as young children. I was annoyed by how blasé some folks can be about the toll these challenges take on our military kiddos.

Fast forward some years, and I've come to realize that our children indeed struggled more than Steve and I comprehended. More than even they realized at the time. A couple of them are still working through their own burdens and trials, and that's their story to tell, not mine. Some of those issues might not be directly linked to military life. Perhaps they would have happened anyway, but as their mom I can't help but wonder what would have been different if they'd enjoyed more stability during their growing-up years. What could we have done better? *Did we miss something?* Military parents or not, no matter how old your kids are, it's hard not to blame yourself when your children go through difficult times. It's so tempting to beat yourself up when your children have struggles.

As much effort and love as we poured into our children over the years, I have to realize I have no control over the outcome. My children are grown now, in their mid-twenties and thirties, and the decisions they make are theirs alone.

As I reflect, I'm reminded no matter what I didn't know when I was raising my children—God knew. God knew exactly the path my children would take, the challenges that would be thrown at them, the choices they would ultimately make. This is comforting for me as a person of faith.

So, to the question, "Will my military kids be okay?" I don't believe there is a pat answer to be had. All parents come to understand that there are no guarantees, no matter how hard you try or how intentional you are. And all we can do is offer our best.

THIS ISN'T THE MOVIES

Steve was dozing in the living room recliner, his back to the window facing the street. Every so often, he'd jump, startled awake by any noise or movement. I left the room to put away laundry and when I came back a few minutes later, he had turned the recliner to face the window with the back against the wall. He was sound asleep and peaceful, lightly snoring. Later when I remarked on his unexpected furniture rearrangement, he told me he couldn't relax when he couldn't see what was going on behind him, even everyday occurrences like cars passing on the street. He'd returned from a deployment to Iraq only a few days before, and the hyper-vigilance and awareness that came with having lived and worked in Baghdad for the preceding months was hard to let go.

I'd picked him up from the airfield on Grand Forks Air Force Base when he came home from this first deployment, a very anticlimactic end to six months apart. No ceremony, no fanfare, just me and the kids rolling up in our minivan in the dark after he called to let me know he'd landed. He was waiting outside the hangar, along with some of the others from his unit who'd also returned, surrounded by footlockers and duffle bags. The kids scrambled out of the van as soon as I stopped and nearly tackled him as he ran to them, his backpack and green duffle bag dropped on the ground behind him. We'd huddled in a group hugging for a few minutes, all of us crying, the relief palpable.

Now, Steve had a couple of weeks off to readjust and rest before returning to his normal duties. I was surprised at how foreign it felt to have him back home after I'd missed him so much, and I wasn't prepared at all for the readjustments we'd each need to make over the coming weeks.

Reintegration is the name given to the time period after a military member returns home from a deployment. According to Military OneSource, "Reunion and reintegration is when service members return home, complete post-deployment recovery and administrative requirements and reintegrate into home station life."[4]

It sounds so straightforward, doesn't it? Deployment over? *Check.* Back with the family that you missed so much? *At last!* Paperwork done? *Good to go!* But conflicting emotions seem to come along for the ride with deployments and military mandated separations.

You're excited to see each other again. You can't wait to be reunited, *but* you've each been through different circumstances, and each has inevitably changed. The service member has experienced stressful and perhaps even traumatic events, some they're not free to discuss with their spouse. The spouse has shouldered the weight of keeping the family together and home life going, likely with few breaks, and may be physically and emotionally exhausted. It's not the honeymoon often portrayed in movies, TV shows, or social media posts. (In fact, military spouses sometimes refer to these over-sentimentalized images and videos as "reunion porn," because they play on people's emotions without portraying the reality of homecoming.) The initial moments of reuniting bring feelings of happiness and relief, of course, but the days, weeks, and even months after can be a complicated and confusing time.

Before Steve's last return from deployment, we talked over the phone several times about how we had a handle on "this reintegration thing" and our eyes wide open to possible problems. We'd been through this before and had been married over twenty years at that point. We knew the tensions that could surface after such a long time apart. We understood we would each need to extend patience and understanding, and yet—we still had to go through it. After the honeymoon period that followed his homecoming, I found myself fuming over the socks he left on the floor, while he questioned certain decisions I'd made while he'd been away.

Lizann Lightfoot, a veteran Marine Corps spouse and the author of *Open When: Letters of Encouragement for Military Spouses*, said no matter how many times you go through it, deployment and reintegration bring unforeseen issues and feelings.

"We went through our seventh deployment ... and there were still new challenges that we hadn't dealt with before," she said. "I think you do get stronger. You do learn your coping mechanisms and routines and whatever is going to work for your family. People think that you get good at it and that it gets easier. I don't think it's really easier. It's just more a matter of we've been through it before, and we know what to expect and we've gotten some things right. But still, you're just lonely. It's still just as difficult and painful."

A longtime Air Force spouse, Terri went through multiple deployments with her husband, Jim, and she also gives voice to the inevitable clash of emotions and expectations.

"I got very used to having to be very, very independent, which is a good trait," Terri said. "But it's not a great trait when they come home and you forget to check in with them like you should, because they do have an opinion, too. They're part of this marriage; they're part of this family."

Reintegration can bring up feelings of confusion, misunderstanding, and even sadness that things aren't going the way you'd envisioned. Homecoming emotions tend to run high, along with surprise that you still feel lonely, which doesn't make sense to you since your person is not across the world any longer but sitting five feet away. There are so many conflicting emotions. Some spouses have admitted feeling guilty that their service member came home when others didn't.

It doesn't have to be a combat mission or a year-long separation to be difficult. Permission to "feel the feels" and acknowledge the difficulties of any separation is important. So is walking a mile in each other's shoes as a couple. Each of you will have challenges.

After my husband's longest deployment, I told him I couldn't imagine being away from our children for a year as he had been. By the same token, he couldn't understand everything I'd been through at home, dealing with all the household tasks, making family decisions, and solo parenting for months on end. To understand each other better, we could try to imagine what it would feel like to be the one far away or the one left behind. It's a good time to lean into each of your strengths and appreciate what the other brings to the relationship.

"Walking in the other person's shoes is so important," said Terri. "I would be thinking, What about my needs? I have been alone; I've done this; I've done that. If you start those little mental tallies, nobody wins. It's not a competition. I've never had to go to the Middle East and be away from my kids and have no one hug me. And if I did go through that, how would I deal with it? And then you suddenly have a lot more grace."

When your spouse is deployed, the time apart will change you both; it's inevitable. It won't be like the movies but keep your hope alive. You can work through these days toward an even better and stronger marriage.

JOURNEY THROUGH PTSD

Military spouses who are veterans themselves are a special group with a unique perspective on military life. Christina is an Army veteran and Air Force spouse who met her husband, Michael, when they were in high school together. She joined the Army National Guard right after graduation and served for eight years, and he joined the Air Force. The two reconnected on social media after she'd left the Army and while he was deployed.

"He told me that the second we reconnected, he knew we'd get married," she said.

Christina came from a military-oriented background with several family members who served, but she was the first female service member in her family. Soon after she completed her training, Christina was sent on a fifteen-month deployment to Iraq. During that time, she experienced events and trauma that marked her life forever and later culminated in a diagnosis of post-traumatic stress disorder. Christina is very open about her journey dealing with post- traumatic stress disorder (PTSD) and how she has gotten to the point where it doesn't control her anymore.

"I *have* PTSD, but I no longer *suffer* from it," she said.

In her deployment, she was in the second wave of soldiers after the invasion of Iraq in 2003. Part of Christina's job was setting up contracting and financing offices all around Iraq, Kuwait, and Qatar.

"I saw a lot, and I was so young," said Christina. Although about half of her unit was female, they didn't live together and were tasked with different jobs, so she said she didn't see them very much. She remembers the fear that was part of her experience in Iraq.

"You're afraid for your life every day," she said. "Trying to stay aware and sane is almost indescribable, but I will say it has helped me now with being a military spouse. I deal with things now and take them in stride and don't freak out so much. I just tell myself, 'It's the military life. It is what it is.'"

After her Iraq deployment, Christina spent the remainder of her eight years of service in a full-time National Guard position. She reflects on being a woman soldier in a male-oriented world:

"You know, it's really hard because [male servicemembers], they're great people, but I think sometimes they see you *only* as a female," she said. "I worked hard to get where I was, but they didn't see that as equal. You can't do the things that they do. So that was a little bit of a battle. I have seen somewhat of a change, especially in the Army, because now so many females are allowed to do those jobs that were male-only jobs when I was in . . . You know, I faced a lot of things and I've come through a lot of things, but they never saw me as being that tough. But my husband will tell others, 'My wife is a bad chick. She's done some things I haven't done.'"

When Christina returned home from her long deployment, she was plagued with recurring nightmares, mood swings, anxiety, and panic attacks. She decided to speak to a therapist about some relationship issues but was surprised when the therapist suggested she might also be dealing with post-traumatic stress. She wasn't convinced initially.

"It took some time for me to realize that's what it was," she said. "Before I left for deployment, I was this happy-go-lucky person. And then when I came home, I was full of anxiety. I was moody and depressed. People just thought that's who I had become. Whereas really, I was suffering with PTSD and didn't know how to handle it. It's kind of a hard pill to swallow that something has affected you so much that it's now affecting your whole life."

Christina said Michael has been her rock as she's worked through the process of managing her PTSD. After they were married for several years, they and their two daughters were stationed overseas. She described having a breakdown in the middle of a crowd and how he supported her.

"We had to drop something off to someone at another base when we lived in Belgium. And instead of going to the base, we told the military member we'd meet them in the city. She ended up running late, and we got stuck in the city for hours with crowds of people. And I had a full-blown panic attack in front of my kids, in front of my husband. I was crying and hysterical, and it was the first time that my husband literally looked at me and was like, *I comprehend fully what you're saying now*. And seeing me break down like that, he got us right out of there. You know, he got me in the car. He got us out of there, and for the rest of the day, I was a mess. I felt horrible because my kids saw it. But in the same aspect, it's a learning experience for all of us to say, 'Okay, this is a serious thing we have to deal with.'"

Communicating her needs to her husband and working with her therapist have been key to Christina's ability to create a fulfilling life in spite of PTSD. She emphasized the importance of getting help when it's needed.

"I still see a therapist. It's not something that you totally recover from and don't need help dealing with," she said. "I don't see a therapist as often anymore because I have my coping mechanisms. It doesn't control me anymore, and it used to control me. I think if I had to stress something, it's that if you do feel you have it, then go talk to someone. I mean, there's no shame in it."

She also stressed the need for honesty with herself and others.

"You don't always see the effects of it, necessarily. A lot of it is internal . . . dealing internally with these different struggles and these different fights," she said. "And the biggest thing they can do is be open and communicate with the other person, like I do with my husband. I used to not talk to him about it. But now, in the last few years, I've opened up more with him about it and what I deal with, and though he doesn't fully comprehend it, I have at least expressed it to him."

As Christina has moved forward over the years and learned to live with PTSD, she has this advice to offer her fellow veterans:

"If you're suffering from PTSD or other issues, please reach out and utilize military resources like Military OneSource. That's how I got my first free counseling appointments, and I can't recommend them enough. My life is totally different than it was even a few years ago. They literally saved my life."

If you are facing issues related to post-traumatic stress or other trauma or are in an abusive or unsafe situation, please seek help. Here are a few of the resources available to you:

- Veteran/Military Crisis Line: Dial 988 and press 1 or text 838255
- National Domestic Violence Hotline: 800-799-SAFE or text "START" to 88788
- Suicide and Crisis Lifeline: Dial 988
- Military OneSource confidential counseling is available for military and family members: 800-342-9647 or through their website.

WHEN YOU'RE WEARY

Steve's voice crackled across the bad connection. I could barely hear what he was saying, so I pressed the phone harder against my head. I covered my other ear to drown out the background noise of my boisterous teens playing a video game.

"*No!* That's not what I said!" I yelled into the phone.

I heard his voice faintly answering back, less distinct than the mumbles of Charlie Brown's teacher, then the line clicked dead. Frustrated, I shook the phone as if it would make the call magically reappear. No such luck. It was doubtful I'd be hearing from him anytime soon, since the call had dropped on his end. *Dang it.* Communication during this deployment had been a challenge because of his austere location.

I looked around our white-tiled home in Germany and tried to envision what was going on where he was in Afghanistan. Video chat wasn't an option where he was deployed, so I could only use my imagination. I visualized dusty camo tents and a barren desert landscape, and the photos he showed me later proved I wasn't far off the mark.

But that day, another problem needed my attention. One of our teens had been in a minor fender bender, and living in Germany added some complications. We kept all our important paperwork filed in a metal lockbox—military families are nothing if not prepared and organized for almost any contingency— but for some reason, I couldn't seem to lay my hands on the insurance papers I needed. Discouraged, I sank onto the loveseat and felt hot tears beginning to push at the corners of my eyes. *Ugh.* This was such a silly thing to cry over. In the preceding months, we'd gone through the unexpected death of a close active-duty friend, leaving us all reeling. Then I'd been flattened by a bad case of pneumonia for about a month. Now, those were events worth shedding tears over, not stupid paperwork.

Angry at this sign of weakness, I brushed the tears aside and turned to the matter at hand. One I'd need to solve alone. Again.

It was a situation easily resolved once I discovered the wayward papers, but in the next few months parenting solo continued to be a challenge. *What was wrong with me?* I'd already been through several long deployments, and I'd stopped counting how many training separations and temporary duty assignments we'd muddled through over the previous twenty-plus years. But with this year-long deployment, a weariness had attached itself to me, one I hadn't anticipated.

Up to this point, I was mostly an "I've got this" type of military spouse. But this deployment was different—more demanding. All four of our children were in their teens, so I carried the weight of driver's ed, dashed teen romances, friend drama, prom, and graduation season alone, thousands of miles from our extended family. Not to mention the added layer that we were all missing Steve and worried over his safety. I could no longer shield the kids from what was going on in the world as I used to do when they were younger. There were moments when I didn't feel I could manage another day, but then a friend would call or drop by with cookies or a casserole. Some days the kids and I would take an impromptu day trip to a nearby country (France and Belgium were so close!) and I'd remind myself of all the good reasons we'd decided to stay overseas when the orders for this latest deployment had come down. I was thankful to live on base, to have access to all the military family support, to be part of the base chapel community, and to have so many people around who truly cared about how we were doing and supported us in so many ways. But still—I was tired.

As autumn gathered steam, we made plans to fly to Texas to spend Christmas break with family. Then I realized another thing I'd be doing alone. *College visits.* Our oldest son

Matthew would graduate before his dad returned, and there were several schools he hoped to visit while we were back in the U.S. Here was one more thing I hadn't anticipated doing without my husband. I knew I could do it. That wasn't the issue. I'd done so many hard things on my own over the years. I'd come to relish my sense of self, my independence, being able to tackle problems head on and solve them myself or figure out where to find needed resources. But as my dad used to say, the "want to" had left me.

REACHING OUT

Jennifer Pasquale, the founder of *Pride & Grit*, a support resource for military spouses, is someone who can relate to this feeling. In an interview for my podcast, *Milspouse Matters*, she gave voice to what many long-time military spouses feel.

"A lot of us have been around a long time, and we've weathered a lot of hard things in military life. We're tired. It's not that we didn't love being a service family, but we were tired. And I noticed that people didn't have a space to be tired that was supportive for them. I call it the 'compounding impact of service.' It's not the second move. The second move is still fun. It's maybe the twelfth move or the ninth move or it's the fourth time you had to give up the job you love because you're following your service member. Sometimes it takes a while for these things to show up. It's like flipping a switch for a lot of folks. For me, it was like that. I was fine until I wasn't. I was good with all the changes, and fine with being what one friend calls 'the trailing spouse.' I was comfortable with that role—until I wasn't."

Now more than ever, there's so much support for military spouses, both new and seasoned. But at the time of Steve's last deployment, there weren't nearly the resources available today. Or if there was, I was too stubborn to admit I needed any of them. So, I did what I always did, stuffed down my frustrations and resentment, forged ahead, figured it out. When we arrived in Texas that Christmas, my dad offered to come along with us for the long drives to visit colleges, and it turned out to be a special time together. Still, in the back of my mind the thought simmered, *Steve should be here for this.*

When we returned to Germany after our long trip back to the States, we discovered that one of the cars wouldn't start. Later that week, the other car broke down, too. Getting your vehicle repaired overseas is not typically straightforward, and here we were with both vehicles useless. I was sick again with bronchitis and could barely get out of bed. While figuring out this latest situation, we received a welcome phone call from Steve. After I explained to him what was going on, he pleaded with me to knock on our neighbor's door and ask for his expertise in car repair. Though I resisted, I had to finally relent and admit I couldn't handle this on my own. Our neighbor helped our son jumpstart one car and drove him to the auto parts store on base to replace some whatsit or gadget in the other. The solution was actually quite simple, but I'd made it more complicated than necessary by my hardheadedness.

I would like to tell you I became better at seeking out help when I needed it, but that wouldn't be true. I really did make attempts to get better at it, but my stubbornness was strong. Thankfully I had some friends who, at times, forced their care and assistance on me, whether I thought I needed it or not.

One such friend was Karen. She lived a few blocks away from me in base housing. Every couple of weeks during Steve's last deployment, my phone would ring, and Karen would announce,

"Greg's firing up the margarita machine! Come on over!"

I'd look around my messy house, at my kids trailing in and out of the door, catch a glimpse of my saggy yoga pants in the streaked bathroom mirror—someone really needed to clean that—and think of an excuse for why I couldn't join them. But

Karen usually wouldn't take no for an answer. She might even ring my doorbell and all but physically compel me to come over.

These invitations were ostensibly for drinks and a chat, but I realize now that Karen recognized when I wasn't doing well or needed a break from the grind of solo parenting. I tried to hide it, but my weariness was showing. And I am so thankful that she was paying attention.

My default mode seems to be one where I plow ahead blindly and exhaust myself. I know plenty of military spouses who are built this way, too. If that's you, let me remind us both it's not a sign of weakness to admit we could use a little help. I learned the hard way that giving myself a break was crucial, and asking for help was not a sign of weakness.

"When you judge yourself for needing help, you judge those you are helping," says author and speaker Brené Brown. "When you attach value to giving help, you attach value to needing help. The danger of tying your self-worth to being a helper is feeling shame when you have to ask for help. Offering help is courageous and compassionate, but so is asking for help."[5]

FINDING JOY AGAIN

Widow. A simple word infused with so many layers of meaning. A huge loss contained in one word. Falling in love, inside jokes, challenges, arguments, making up after arguments, and all the years together. Then the unspeakable heartbreak when half of yourself is no more.

How can the devastating blow of losing your partner, of all that you thought your future would be, all that it should be—how can that be forced into one little word? But here we are. Years of memories, of loss, of a future changed. At times, the English language fails in expressing completely the true meaning behind a word, and that is the case with this one word: widow.

"No one ever told me that grief felt so like fear," wrote C.S. Lewis after the death of his wife, Joy. "I am not afraid, but the sensation is like being afraid. The same fluttering in the stomach, the same restlessness, the yawning. I keep on swallowing. At other times it feels like being mildly drunk, or concussed. There is a sort of invisible blanket between the world and me. I find it hard to take in what anyone says. Or perhaps, hard to want to take it in. It is so uninteresting. Yet, I want the others to be about me. I dread the moments when the house is empty. If only they would talk to one another and not to me."[6]

Something I've learned from talking to so many military widows is that there's no right way to grieve, and it's never wise to put grief on a timetable. Each person has to deal with their own grief as it ebbs and flows. It's something we face, not something we "get over."

"You never get over losing your spouse," one widow told me. "It becomes part of you, and you learn how to live in spite of it. When people tell you that you're doing it wrong, walk away from them."

My friend Chris lost her husband Lonnie some years ago, and I have been inspired by her grace in the face of such immeasurable loss.

Chris is one of those people who makes you feel like an immediate friend. Happy, positive, and smiling, she is the first to offer help to anyone who needs it. She is also a gifted musician. When we met in the early 2000s, she played the piano and led worship at Andersen AFB chapel in Guam where her husband, Lonnie, was one of the chaplains. Her youngest was a high schooler then, and my oldest was just beginning eighth grade. Chris was an experienced homeschooling mom of four who gave me much inspiration for homeschooling my own four children.

In one of the happy coincidences of military life, we were stationed together again in Germany nearly a decade later. We were part of their weekly Bible study, and my kids were thrilled to pick back up with their favorite piano teacher.

By that time, Chris and Lonnie had spent more than twenty years as a military family, raising their four children across the world. They'd weathered deployments, the constant changes of military life. Their children had all grown up, married, had children, and lived in various places back in the States. Lonnie and Chris loved spending time with their family. Their home was much like the many quilts Chris crafted by hand: warm, welcoming, and a place to nestle in and find comfort.

With an eye on Lonnie's upcoming retirement from the Air Force, they were making plans to buy a house and settle in Montana, Chris's home state. They looked forward to the days when they'd have more time to spend with their grown children and growing brood of grandchildren.

But on a dark November night, Lonnie died unexpectedly at age fifty-three. In one swift moment of loss, Chris's future took a hard turn from the course they had planned together to one in which she'd have to claw her way out of the darkness alone to return to the simple tasks of living.

One of my own memories from the time after Lonnie's death was Chris's concern for others. In the hours after he died, some friends brought her to their home so she wouldn't be alone while she waited for her oldest son and his wife to arrive on a flight from the U.S. In the middle of the flurry of activity and paperwork that comes in the aftermath of a service member's death, other friends had gathered to sit with her when they'd heard the news. Chris had been speaking with the casualty assistance officer (CAO), and he was getting up to leave. The CAO is the person assigned by the military to be a support and guide to surviving family members as they deal with all the unwanted tasks and decisions that must be made. The CAO also ensures the family's immediate needs are provided for after a military member's death. Of course, being overseas brought other complications and details like transporting the body and arranging funeral services back in the States. Chris had already spent some time with the CAO that day, trying to take in some of the details of what would happen next. Her Lonnie had been alive mere hours earlier, and now she would need to think about planning his funeral. But as the CAO turned to slip out of the room, Chris stopped him, her hand on his arm.

"I just don't want this to make you doubt God's love for you," she said. She looked around the room and said it again, to all the friends who'd gathered around to share their own grief and to support her. "Do not let what happened change your view of how much God loves you," she repeated to us.

It was stunning that she could think about anyone else at that moment. *She* was comforting *us*.

Years later, Chris told me how she felt God's comfort so strongly during that time as grief threatened to overwhelm her after Lonnie's death. The military community overseas is a close one, and many friends came alongside to support her. Chris had the grace to allow others to come into her space and offer comfort. She said one friend insisted she not spend the first night after Lonnie's death alone. The friend slept in the same room with her, simply saying, "I'm here if you need me." It meant so much to Chris, though it was not something she even realized she needed.

"Just to know that even in the midst of the worst of the worst of times, that God's love is there for us," said Chris. "It was just poured out by the people around me. The youth group from Germany came to where I was staying after Lonnie died, and they surrounded the house to pray for me. I didn't see them do it, but I heard that they had done this prayer circle. One thing that was so important was how people were just there for me. They'd just be there and sit with me. They didn't feel like they had to have the answers."

STEADFAST LOVE

As her friends, other service members, and families came to express their condolences, one friend, a general officer, stopped to give her a hug and whispered into her ear the promise from the third chapter of Lamentations: "The steadfast love of the Lord never changes. His mercies never come to an end. They are new every morning. Great is Thy faithfulness."

Still, Chris worried how her family would deal with the untimely death of their father and grandfather. She surrounded herself with her faith community. Slowly, she began making plans for what would come next. Baby steps on the long journey of grief.

Chris traveled back to the U.S. for Lonnie's funeral services and to spend time with her children, grandchildren, and friends. When she returned to Germany a couple of months later to prepare her car and household goods for transport back to the U.S., she had a taste of God's providence.

"So many special things happened. I felt like God was showing his presence to me," said Chris. "Lonnie used to speak about the 'precious promise of God's presence' in our life. And there was a phrase he often used about keeping our eyes on eternity, realizing that it's all about keeping the eyes of our hearts set on eternal life. And there were things that God did for us that were just incredible. When I went back to Germany months later to close out my house with my friend Terry, I had to get my car and make sure it was all cleaned out so it could be shipped. There was one piece of paper in my car, a bulletin from a Sunday in the previous July where Lonnie had spoken. So, it had pre-printed verses, and one of the verses was highlighted. But I didn't know it. The wind swept the paper out of my hand, underneath the car. So, I ran around to the side, and it was in January, so there was snow everywhere. I was looking for a white piece of paper on the white ground and all of a sudden, I saw it fluttering, so I picked it up. I took it inside the house, and I was just looking at this piece of paper and that verse. It was almost—you know how sometimes you look at words and it's like they're highlighted. And there was that same verse from Lamentations the general had spoken to me. To me, it was just another reminder. God was reminding me . . . after everything that yes, the steadfast love of the Lord never changes. I couldn't believe it."

Chris recalled a memory from her growing up years in Montana. She lost her parents at a young age and her life had already been marked by grief and pain.

"I remember as a young person in Miles City, Montana, riding my bike down the middle of the street and singing at the top of my lungs, 'The joy of the Lord is my strength.'" Chris said. "And now my son Jeremy, every night when he puts his boys to bed, they all say that verse together as they say their prayers before going to sleep at night. And I have that verse hanging on my bathroom wall. In the difficult times, you don't even understand it, you can feel like there's no joy whatsoever. And I just pray, whatever that means, 'the joy of the Lord is my strength,' that God somehow gives us what we need for each day, as we seek him, and trust in him, and hope in the future. It's not dependent on any kind of joy that I can conjure up. That verse just seems to have always been one of my life verses."

Chris's eyes well up with tears at times when she talks about Lonnie. And she continues to make it a practice of choosing joy daily, to take one step forward at a time.

Choose joy. That's all she can do.

PART 4

FRIENDSHIP STORIES

GROWING STRONGER TOGETHER

I would rather walk with a friend in the dark,
than alone in the light. —Helen Keller

My tiny baby boy lay in a crib festooned with a plastic oxygen tent. Steve and I had spent the night at the hospital, finding simple comfort in observing his breathing, watching his little chest going up and down, up and down. Through my sleep-deprived, dazed thoughts, the beeping of the IVs and machines that monitored his breathing and heart rate kept a steady rhythm. That was good. Better than the alarms that had gone off in the previous hours, causing medical staff to come running into the room.

When Gabriel's condition seemed more stable, Steve had headed home to shower, pack me an overnight bag, and check on our two-year-old, who was with a sitter. As I sat alone, fear blanketed my thoughts and held my heart in a grip icier than the January winds blowing outside the hospital room. I felt helpless, like I should be doing something active to protect my baby—something, *anything*, to help him get well.

Gabriel was such a plump, happy infant, it seemed impossible that he could be so ill. The knowledge that he was getting the best care possible was a comfort, albeit a small one. He was only five months old and suffering a serious case of pneumonia which, though we didn't know at the time, would reveal he had reactive airways that would require frequent breathing treatments and close monitoring of his condition for the next several years.

We were stationed in Ohio, hundreds of miles from our nearest family back home in New Mexico. Into my fog of fear and exhaustion walked a friend and fellow military wife. She lived down the street from the base hospital and had left her own small children with a neighbor so she could take a few moments to check on us. She found me, sitting beside Gabriel's hospital crib.

"I'm here. How can I help?"

I looked at her uncomprehendingly. She sat down beside me, still in her wool coat, and pressed a peanut butter and jelly sandwich into my hands. I breathed in the cold she brought from the wintry world outside. How crazy to think there was life beyond this hospital room. Realizing how hungry I was under my thick layer of fatigue, I began unwrapping the sandwich. A simple PB&J had never looked so good.

"I'm sorry, it's all I had," she said, "and I figured you might be hungry."

I took a bite and closed my eyes as I savored the homey offering. We'd been at the hospital nearly twenty-four hours, and she was the first person who'd entered our crisis with us. I wanted to tell her she didn't need to bring me anything, that just having someone there who cared about us was enough, but the words didn't come. Instead, I leaned my head against her shoulder and burst into tears as the weight of the past hours fell away for a brief moment.

"Oh honey, it's gonna be okay," she soothed. "It's gonna be okay."

She put her arm around me and shushed me like a small child. I realized then how lucky I was to have a friend willing to sit with me in hard moments that have no answers.

Friend. What a loaded word. Some of us have a best friend we've known since kindergarten, others struggle to make or keep friends, while the lucky ones seem to make friends wherever they go. Life can give us mixed messages about friends and how much we need them. Studies show that those with significant relationships suffer lower rates of depression and that, "to age well, you need friends."[1]

But we also are told, perhaps especially in military life, that we need to stand on our own two feet, be independent, and handle things on our own. And while we might be able to, why would we want to when we don't have to? In difficult times and in good times, as a military spouse, I've often found comfort in having a friend by my side.

Years after Gabriel's hospital stay, when we were stationed at Ramstein, Germany, I was at a St. Patrick's Day celebration. I stood on tiptoe at the edge of the crowd, craning to see my girls march out with their Irish dancing group. Steve had recently deployed, and both of my older teens were at their after-school jobs. So, I stood alone, solo-parent style, as I often did.

Suddenly, my friend Christy appeared at my elbow.

"Are we too late?" she asked breathlessly. Stunned, I looked past Christy to see her husband and another friend Amy and *her* husband. Tears sprang to my eyes as I made room for them.

"We wouldn't have missed this for the world!" Amy sang out.

Families get busy with their own lives. I know how busy mine gets. But these families knew how much my girls were missing their daddy and took time out of *their* busy Saturday to watch *my* kids make their way through their first Irish dance performance—with the biggest smiles on their faces when they spotted our friends with me in the crowd. I will love those friends forever for that.

I grew up near an Air Force base, and military families moved in and out of our town. Some of them became my closest friends, but I never thought about how hard it must have been for them to start over each time they moved. Again, and again.

Now, I get it.

I know what it feels like to constantly be new, to feel alone though surrounded by people. To wonder, *Will I make a friend here? Or will this be a duty station I just get through?* I've felt the paralyzing insecurity, awkwardness, and loneliness, trying to trust that it will get better, like it always has—but in the moment, it just *really, really sucks*. I wish I could gather up all my wonderful friends from around the world and fill up a room with them and sit. And visit.

With no goodbyes.

That would be the best.

SAY GOODBYE TO SAY HELLO

As military spouses we're often in a location for only a few years—and sometimes making friends hardly seems worth the effort. It can be challenging to get to know someone, and even more difficult to know that when you do find a kindred spirit, you'll likely be saying goodbye soon.

In spite of the difficulties, in spite of the times I got close to someone right before one of us moved, or even those locations where I couldn't seem to connect, I've learned that friendship is still worth the effort. The gain of making friends is worth the pain of goodbye.

Relationships. Who can guess the magnitude of the meaning they'll hold in our hearts until we look back on our lives? A small kindness becomes enormous to the person receiving it when it's so desperately needed. Sure, we can get by on our own—until the moment we can't. As we recognize our need for friendship, may we be aware of those around us who could use a kind word, a simple acknowledgment. May we take the time to ask, "How are you doing, *really*?" And may we also remember to be open to receiving those small kindnesses ourselves. Sometimes, that's the most difficult part.

Well, almost. Saying goodbye is painful too—for us and our children.

"Miss Tara! Don't leeeave meee!" wailed five-year-old Grace, stretching out her arms to my friend Tara and her family as we said our last farewells before leaving Florida to move to Guam.

Her cries were heart rending. Though Grace was born in Texas, our life and friends in Florida were all the life and friends she could remember. She was leaving behind everything familiar, and the final goodbye to my friend Tara had put her—and me—over the top.

As we drove away from Tara's house, I bit my lip and turned my face to the car window, attempting to hide the tears that burned down my cheeks as we drove away. My kids were already upset about this move, and I didn't want to add to their distress. And I was so tired of goodbyes.

When I used to visit my Nana in New Mexico and it was time to say goodbye, she would always say, "You can't say hello again without saying goodbye." In fact, she said it the last time I saw her before she passed away.

Over the years of forced goodbyes from family and friends, we learned to start saying, "See you later," as a reminder that we might cross paths or be stationed together again one day. The military world gets smaller the longer you're in it. Still, no matter what words we choose when we part, it still hurts.

Military families move ten times more often than their civilian counterparts[2] and with a small percentage of the U.S. population serving on active duty, there's often a divide of understanding between what military families experience and what civilians may perceive. From the outside, it can look like an exciting lifestyle of globetrotting and travel for military families moving all over the world, and it does have its perks. Still, the process of leaving behind beloved friendships and networks and rebuilding them in a new place every few years can be one of the most challenging aspects of military life.

This mobility adds complications to family separations, when the active-duty member is away for a deployment, training, or other temporary duty assignments. One of the significant differences between military deployments now and those of twentieth century wars is that in the past, military families were more likely to live near their extended families. Military members were of course gone for long periods of time, in World War II for example, but their families were more likely to be located near a stable network of grandparents, aunts, uncles, and friends, rather than stationed somewhere far from home.

In the years following the Vietnam conflict, a more mobile military began deploying out of stateside installations and leaving families behind at locations where they were assigned. This began the experience of move-deploy-move-deploy that so many of today's military families know so well.[3] We may understand the reasons for moving military members from place to place—fulfilling mission requirements, receiving location-specific training or education, preventing stagnation in leadership, and so on. Sure, we understand, but even good reasons can ring a bit hollow when we are pulling up stakes to move our families again.

IT'S STILL CRAZY

Today's military families do have better support than past generations, and family stability is recognized as important to the military mission. However, it's still a crazy way for families to live, this constant uprooting and replanting, all while saying goodbye to the active-duty member for months or even years at a time as they deploy.

As my own family experienced moves and deployments, I've learned that friends can be what make even an austere location bearable and a lonesome deployment less lonely. When memories of hardship fade, the memories and benefits of relationships will remain. Friends have tended to my children while I was ill or having surgery, especially when Steve was deployed or TDY—and friends can help in smaller ways, too. I once drove across town to a friend's house late at night while her husband was deployed to check her porch and make sure the frightening sound she was hearing was not a burglar. It was just the wind blowing a tree branch against her window, I reassured her. That's what friends do.

When we were stationed in Texas, I was placed on bedrest with a complicated pregnancy, when my other three children were six years old and under. My friend Kim arrived at my door one afternoon, announcing that she was there to clean my bathrooms. She didn't wait to be asked; she just showed up. She scrubbed the holy heck out of the sinks, tubs, and toilets while I lay on the couch with tears running down my cheeks, humbled by her kindness. Again, that's what friends do. They show up. They ease our fears and lighten our loads.

Kim and I met in Ohio when our kids were all small, stayed in touch after multiple moves, then reconnected years later when we were both stationed in Germany—each of our homes full of teens by that point. Though we've been long distance friends for a couple of decades now, time and distance make no difference when it comes to "bosom friends," to quote *Anne of Green Gables*. I have been greatly blessed by these life-long friendships with military spouses. People who share your mission and way of life may be the most loyal friends you'll ever make.

Many of us have learned from frequent moves and time spent apart from our spouses that we aren't guaranteed a long time to wait for friendship to slowly blossom. We may have to speed up the process. Some of my best friends are those that I knew "in real life" for a *year*. One. Year.

This is especially true in overseas and remote assignments. As I mentioned, during our time living in Guam, we endured several natural disasters including typhoons and earthquakes. These were traumatic experiences for most of the military families stationed there, as those events upended the expectations of normal life, such as dependable electricity and potable water. You become friends quickly when sharing gas rations for generators, scrubbing out laundry together with bottled water, or finding creative ways to keep toddlers occupied and cool in tropical heat and humidity—without electricity.

Shared hardships have a way of forging the best of friendships, especially when you have no family nearby to lean on. But it's not only the hard times that bond us. While living in Germany, I joined forces with other military spouses eager to explore Europe.

We took USO trips to nearby locations like the Netherlands and Switzerland and day trips to local markets. We bonded over our lackluster, yet sincere, attempts at ordering food in German at a local café, and seeking a restroom—a sort of *Where's Waldo?* search—while on a walking tour of a small village.

When we were stationed in Washington, DC, I met several fellow military spouses at a homeschooling group. We decided to get together for a weekly book club, which quickly devolved into less talking about books and more sharing about our lives over coffee. When I look back at it now, it's surprising how quickly we bonded over those few months of shared caffeine, laughter, and chat. Or maybe it's not so surprising. I value the friends who've given me a glimpse into their hearts and lives.

I recently overheard a conversation between two women in the civilian community where I live now.

"Yeah, we've only been here a year," said one. "It takes that long to get settled in before you get to know people."

This is not always the case for military spouses. We know time is limited, so we tend to cut right to the chase when it comes to seeking out and making friends. That doesn't mean it's always easy. I don't take for granted the offered hand of friendship, because I've lived in enough places where it wasn't extended.

We all crave real, authentic friendship. Though we all go through seasons where real friends can seem difficult to find, I've found it's important to hold onto the hope that you will find your own community. These words from C.S. Lewis may ring true for you as they have for me: "Friendship . . . is born at that moment when one person says to another: 'What! You too? . . . I thought I was the only one.'"[4]

Friends also help keep us healthy. Studies show that those with active friendships live longer than those without a circle of friends.[5] I've learned so much from my sweet friends across the years, including how to be transparent, how to laugh at ridiculous circumstances, when to shut up and when to speak, and most of all, how much I need these wonderful people in my life!

"This all sounds well and good," you might respond. "But I just moved here and don't know a soul."

I've been there. And so have so many others. We know far too well the feeling of loneliness when the dust settles after a move, your kids and spouse are caught up with their own activities, new schools, and busy schedules, and you haven't found your place or landed a job yet, and there you sit—alone. But you don't have to stay that way.

Yes, it stinks to say goodbye to the best friend you've ever had and be forced to start over again. It's exhausting to lay the groundwork for friendships and community connections, knowing it's most likely temporary anyway. Sometimes it seems easier to just—not. But one thing I wish I could tell my past "younger me" is to make room for new friends even if they don't resemble any friend I've ever had before. I've learned I don't have to wait for others to make the first move. Sometimes I have to be the one to take the first brave step toward friendship.

In the years since my husband's retirement from the military, I have missed the instant camaraderie that comes from the shared experiences with other military spouses, the ones who have been there. We share a unique language, sometimes a dark sense of humor cultivated in response to realities like

Murphy and his "deployment curse." The mutual understanding we share is hard to replicate.

Relationships are so important in this lonely world. Whether it's an "in real life" friend, like a friend who will wait with you for news at the hospital, an acquaintance who becomes a friend as you volunteer and serve the community together, or a social network that comes together to support you while your spouse is deployed, we all need friends.

I have definitely learned that some lifelong friendships can survive the years and the miles of separation, and saying goodbye isn't always forever. Sometimes you will say "hello, again" to precious friends. More often you will say "hello" to new ones.

Either way, my Nana's words are still true: "You can't say hello again without saying goodbye."

UNLIKELY FRIENDS

In military life, you will meet people who don't agree with me or my Nana. I experienced this early on. At our first assignment, I crossed paths with a senior spouse at the gym and ventured to ask her about upcoming spouse events, but she told me she wasn't interested in any of that. After "doing this thing for twenty years," as she put it, she said she was tired of goodbyes. Also, she found it hard to know who she could trust, so her solution was not to trust anyone. Her next statement stunned me.

"I don't make friends," she said flatly.

At that point, I'd been married to my airman husband for a grand total of about two years and still didn't know much about military life yet, much less identified with being a "military spouse."

While I didn't know much about military life, I felt a bit sorry for her. She was pleasant, except for her pre-emptive announcement that I didn't need to get my hopes up because we *would not* be friends. Over the next few months, I noticed she kept everyone at arm's length. I don't know what happened that led her to that decision. Perhaps she went through some deep hurt at some point or was just plain weary. Now, I know that look in her eyes. I've seen it more than once in the years since, but I didn't recognize it then. I hope she made peace and was able to let others in somehow.

With the passing of (ahem) a lot of years, I can understand the feelings she expressed, but I've never been able to follow through and "just say no" to friends. As a people person at heart, I don't think I'm capable of it, actually. But I get it.

The hurt of saying goodbye doesn't get easier the more you do it; it gets harder. Probably because you discover how final it can be. The urge to cocoon myself in a self-protective shell is strong, to guard myself from being forced to say goodbye yet again.

But I've been blessed with so many different friends over the years. I would hate to have missed out on any of them. I've become fast friends with women I wouldn't have expected to hit it off with. Twenty years older than me or—now that I'm the older one—many years younger. They're businesswomen, moms with master's degrees or high school diplomas, all manner of political leanings, different religions, and different backgrounds. A beautiful array of friends.

One friend who became especially dear to me was Joy. It didn't seem we had much in common when I first met her at our first assignment, though we were both military spouses. She was the mother of five young children, while I was a twenty-two-year-old registered nurse with no kids. In those days, I worked the night shift at the downtown hospital and picked up take-out food most evenings. I spent my spare time hitting the gym and tanning bed several times a week. Meanwhile, Joy was a stay-at-home homeschooling mom who ground her own flour from wheat berries from a local organic co-op and baked homemade bread every week for her large family. Somehow, in spite of our differences we hit it off. She had a wicked sense of humor and was about a decade ahead of me in military life. She took a very pragmatic view on all things military related, while I was still intimidated by the sight of a lot of stripes on a sleeve or shoulder bling.

We met at church one week, when Steve and I sat in front of Joy, her husband, and their kids. It was the beginning of an unexpected, unlikely, beautiful friendship. Joy found out we were new to the church and quickly invited us to join her and her husband at a small group Bible study for young married couples. Over the next couple of years, I met up with Joy not only for Bible study, but also for lunches she hosted at her home (that homemade bread was so *yummy*), park dates where we sat on a bench and visited while her kids played, and women's church events.

When we had our first baby, Matthew, she brought us delicious meals and gave me so much gentle advice about being a new mom. And when our second baby, Gabriel, was so ill, it was Joy who came to sit with me in the hospital, offering hope, comfort, and a peanut-butter-and-jelly sandwich. She was also the friend who sat with me in silence after I suffered my first miscarriage. No words necessary, just a comforting presence. And after we moved from that duty station, Joy and I kept in touch for years through good old-fashioned handwritten letters.

That was thirty years ago, but I will always remember Joy's kindness to the young, ignorant military spouse that I was. She shared life lessons through her gentle example and casual conversations, and never made me feel stupid. I recognize now in hindsight what a gift she was to me, and how much I learned from her. I'm not quite certain what I brought to the friendship, though perhaps maybe she recognized something of her younger self in me.

Relationships can be messy and difficult. Not all are as easy and organic as my unlikely friendship with Joy. I recognize that, and over the years, I've also experienced friendships that were not so healthy. I've met people who I thought would be amazing but ended up not being a great connection. Some could even fit that overused description toxic. Yes, we've all been there. I've encountered other military spouses who, like that older spouse I met early on, were not open to friendships. They've made the decision that they've been burned too many times, said too many goodbyes, and that it wasn't worth it to them. If that's you, I hope you'll step back a little, let your scorched wings cool off and find the strength to try again.

I'm rooting for you because friendship is worth it.

And you're worth knowing.

WELCOME TO MAYBERRY

Beale Air Force Base, California, is one of those locations you can't really picture until you arrive. When you first learn that you'll be stationed in California, thoughts of the beach, surfboards, and balmy weather might spring to mind.

But Beale is not in that part of California. It's north of Sacramento in a mostly rural area. Depending on which way you approach the base, you'll either be greeted by the tiny town of Linda or the beautiful views of the Sierra Nevada foothills. At the end of our road trip from North Dakota to our new assignment at Beale, we arrived via the Nevada side and were treated to gorgeous views as we made our way down the mountain. Our family of six traveled in a caravan of sorts that included my minivan and Steve's truck, each pulling a small U-Haul trailer. In the preceding days, we'd wended our way through Montana and Idaho before facing down the mountains and unexpected late spring snows of Nevada. Later, other spouses who arrived from the other direction told me how they'd cried at the sight of the somewhat battered brown landscape. But my first impression was of rugged mountains and lush, green meadows as we descended into the foothills.

The base itself is vast. When we were stationed there, parcels of wide-open land on the installation were leased out to area ranchers for grazing their cattle. On my daily jaunts on the many walking trails that crisscrossed the base, I was delighted to watch the cows peacefully ruminating while a U-2—the high-altitude reconnaissance aircraft nicknamed "The Dragon Lady"—rose gracefully from the runway nearby. Flocks of turkey also populated the base, and wandering deer nibbled the rose bushes in front of our home. It was an intriguing mix of worlds, the rural and the high tech.

We signed for the keys to our base housing and received our shipment of household goods a few short weeks after arriving at Beale. One warm spring morning, I stood in our small military house and surveyed the mountain of boxes still waiting to be unpacked when the doorbell rang. Opening the door, I was surprised to find a cluster of children waiting on our porch, shuffling around nervously. Their leader, a freckled girl of about thirteen, stepped forward boldly and asked,

"Do you have kids?"

I didn't even have a chance to answer. My own four, who'd rushed to the door behind me as soon as they'd heard the doorbell, spilled out onto the porch and quickly began comparing notes with their new friends, because that's they were, instantly. Within minutes, the gang headed out to our backyard, which was fenceless and joined with a long field behind the house, ending in a stream that flowed behind the military housing community.

"Don't go too far!" I called after them in vain.

Pretty soon, the arrival of children knocking on the door each afternoon to ask if mine could "come out and play" became a daily occurrence. The echo of the trampoline thumping in the back, the basketball beating a rhythm against the backboard out front, giggling girls creating a Littlest Pet Shop village under the covered porch—it all became part of the happy soundtrack for those spring afternoons and evenings. When retreat and the national anthem were played on the base loudspeakers to mark the end of the duty day, I'd see my children and their friends stop—in the middle of a game of pick-up football or bouncing around on the trampoline—and stand at attention, hands over hearts.

My children, whose ages ranged from mid-elementary through eighth grade by then, each quickly found a friend in the group. As time went on and friendships solidified, I'd only need to glance out my back door in the afternoons to spot my kiddos. Often, I'd field a phone call from a fellow mom telling me the group was headed my way. If I couldn't locate one of my younger children, I'd look out the window over the kitchen sink, see the large bushes shaking, and know that they were involved in playing an elaborate game of "fort" with their friends.

Living on base at Beale seemed like going back in time to Mayberry, the idyllic town from *The Andy Griffith Show*. There were many stay-at-home moms in the neighborhood, and a large homeschooling group organized field trips and classes. Our kids joined the children's choir at the base chapel, and we added community events like fall festivals and spring fun runs to the calendar.

We almost missed all this by choosing to live in a civilian neighborhood when we moved to Beale. We'd spent the previous few assignments living in varied iterations of military housing, from ancient and crumbling to brand new, but our higher housing allowance in California meant we had more options. We'd toured several rental homes in nearby communities. I was bowled over when we stopped by the open house for a large home in a planned neighborhood development. It was stunning, with the latest amenities and kitchen upgrades I'd only dreamed of having. Along with that, there were enough bedrooms for each of our four children to have their own, plus multiple living spaces. This house was expansive compared to the shoebox military housing we'd become accustomed to. At one point during the home tour with the real estate agent, we couldn't find our youngest, Anna, who was about seven years old. We called her name repeatedly, and finally she came tumbling out of a door under the staircase, squealing, "I found a tunnel!"

After the house tour, I penciled notes in my home-rental-tour notebook about the things we could do with more space than we'd ever had. I dreamed of a craft room for me and a separate homeschool room for the children. Steve and I could watch TV in one living area, unbothered and in charge of the remote, while the kids entertained themselves in the other living room or loft. What luxury! Our boys were getting into the gangly teen phase, both nearly six feet tall. My time seemed divided between refilling the fridge and pantry and replacing outgrown clothing. Having room to spread out made sense to my mind. But when we asked our children what they thought about the house off base, ten-year-old Grace burst into tears. I was so confused.

What could possibly be wrong with this house?

It was in a brand-new community, with more homes under construction nearby. The surrounding neighborhood did look a bit barren with newly poured sidewalks and no real trees, only saplings planted here and there. The nearest stores were miles away.

The other children joined Grace's protests about the possibility of living there. They referred to the large home as a "mansion." And not in a complimentary way, more of a "how could you expect us to live in this museum?" way.

They peppered us with questions.

"How will I get to the library? What about the shoppette? And where is the pool?"

And it hit me. By this point in their lives, living in military housing was all our kids could remember. It was their hometown, their security. They were used to having the shoppette, the military's equivalent of a convenience store, within a short walk from home. They loved being able to go alone with their friends to grab a snack or drink. Base amenities we used often, like the pool, gym, bowling alley, and library, were also typically located near housing. Even when we moved, the familiarity of living on base meant a lot to them. My husband suggested a family vote, and mine was the lone hand raised for the big new "mansion." The majority prevailed. Base housing it would be. I looked back longingly at the beautiful home as we pulled away from the curb. *Maybe someday.*

So, we settled into an ancient base house, which—though we didn't know it at the time—would be condemned after we moved out. It was easily a third the size of the home we'd declined off base. It was not new, nor cute. It had old appliances, a floor that shuddered in protest when we walked across it, peeling linoleum, and more—or less. It was just old, but with none of the character of an actual historic home. *Sigh.*

But what it lacked in curb appeal, our rickety military house made up in community. The instant friendships, the neighborhood that so lovingly enfolded us as soon as we arrived was of far greater value than new appliances and extra bedrooms. Steve was sent on a deployment mere months after we moved in, and I was thankful to be surrounded by a caring community that checked on us regularly while he was away.

And one afternoon after we'd unpacked all the boxes and settled in, as the sun set, the familiar strains of the Star-Spangled Banner echoed across the little military housing community. I watched as our kids and their friends paused mid-jump on the trampoline to stand at attention, hands over hearts until the anthem finished playing.

And I knew we'd made the right choice.

NOBODY'S PERFECT

Not all military neighbors are a perfect fit, of course. There will always be some people you're glad to say goodbye to when PCS orders arrive. In an earlier experience with military housing, we had a neighbor who was openly disdainful of the fact that I homeschooled our children, then in grades ranging from kindergarten to sixth grade. This neighbor often made unsolicited comments about my qualifications to homeschool, asked prying questions about my kids' test scores or current coursework, and made passive-aggressive—or maybe just aggressive—remarks about the superiority of public schools over home education. I never asked for her opinion, and I did my best to avoid the topic altogether. Eventually, she decided to avoid us by pretending we didn't exist, a commitment I couldn't help but admire a little, since ignoring a family of six is quite an undertaking.

Even then, I recognized there were surely other issues at play in her life, and there was little I could do to simply get along with her. That just happens sometimes.

This was the only time (as far as I know) that a neighbor hated me at first sight. Living in military housing usually equals fairly close quarters, and unusual lifestyle choices can seem magnified by proximity. Shared common walls, shared yards, can make you feel you have little privacy.

We once had a neighbor who played his giant drum set at all hours in his garage with the door raised, creating quite a racket in the adjoining houses. When asked if he could modify his hours or perhaps close said garage door, he refused.

"Feel free to call the housing office if you don't like it," he said. Not a stellar way to get along with your neighbors. Another neighboring family regularly let their giant dog do its giant business all over our shared backyard.

(Names and locations withheld to protect the annoying.)

On the other hand, we've had wonderful neighbors whose children became fast friends with our own kids. Some are still in touch years later as young adults. Precious military neighbors celebrated with us when we brought home our newborn babies. Others offered support when Steve was deployed, as we gladly did for them in return.

The good memories of friends and neighbors in our years of living in military housing far outweigh the bad.

Military housing in Florida on MacDill AFB meant I lived two blocks from my best friend Tara, and we'd push our double strollers to the pool together most summer afternoons. Housing in North Dakota included a fully finished basement with tons of extra space—handy for the long cold winters—

and was close to the youth center where the kids could meet friends to play basketball or take classes. MacDill was where our older two children held their first jobs, delivering newspapers in the early morning in the relative safety of military housing. Living in military housing in California and Germany meant parks and baseball fields were a short walk or drive away, and friends gathered on crisp fall Sundays to play impromptu games of ultimate frisbee.

At our first assignment in Ohio, our next-door neighbors ended up being some of our best friends. Both Tracy and I were brand new moms. We'd compare notes on our babies' growth spurts and teething woes or knock on the door for an egg or a forgotten cup of sugar we needed for a recipe.

One of the biggest benefits of living in military housing was being surrounded by a community who truly understood what we were going through. Spouse gone for months at a time or back and forth on temporary duty trips like a ping-pong ball? No explanation needed for my military neighbors. At times, living in military housing can feel like the proverbial fishbowl but even so, I found people to be more supportive than not.

During one of Steve's deployments, I was having an especially difficult time with missing him and handling all the kid stuff alone. Maybe my friend picked up on the strained tone of my voice over the phone, or possibly one of my children dropped an innocent clue while playing with her kids. One way or another, as a fellow traveler of the deployment journey, she read the signs. She and another friend surprised me one evening by showing up at my door with a bottle of wine and a DVD of *Nacho Libre*.

"Time for some laughs!" she announced. And she was right. I was grateful for the easy proximity of other military spouse friends who understood.

And talk about feeling secure. There's nothing like driving up to the security gate, seeing the uniformed and armed military police, perhaps even a K-9 unit, to make you feel safe. After Steve retired, leaving the familiarity of military housing was one of the most surprising challenges for me. I'd lived on Air Force bases around the world for decades, and it had become my comfort zone.

And yet, as I surveyed the home we bought in a civilian community after Steve's military retirement, I couldn't help but beam at the privacy, the spaciousness, and the fences that delineated yards and boundaries.

IT'S NOT A GARDEN PARTY

"Two lemonades, please!"

I filled two white foam cups with crushed ice, added lemonade to the brims, and handed them to a dad and his young daughter. The little girl hopped up and down excitedly. Her headband sprouted two springy antennae, topped with sequined red, white, and blue hearts that bobbled up and down as she jumped. She had been to the face-painting booth and had an American flag on one cheek, a little smeared now from swiping her blond hair out of her face. The hot July day had me wiping the sweat off my own face as I stepped back to survey our spouse group's booth, serving up lemonade at Ramstein's Independence Day celebration.

In the booth next to ours, smoke billowed from grills where the Senior NCO organization, Top Three, prepared dozens of brats and burgers. Live country music spilled from speakers overhead, as throngs of military families and civilian guests milled among the booths serving up an international variety of festival food: *Schwenksteak, lumpia,* funnel cakes, cotton candy, and more. The aromas that wafted and mingled in the air made my stomach growl. Maybe I could take a break soon. I chuckled at the sight of a long line that wound around the dunking booth, where many were trying their luck at dousing the base commander. Sitting precariously atop a small metal seat above a tank of water, he wasn't wet—yet.

"Jen, we need you!"

My friend Linda snapped me back to attention to the thirsty people in line at our booth. I'd walk around and explore later. For now, I needed to get back to work selling lemonade to raise money for our spouse group's scholarship fund and events like the monthly Deployment Buddy program we sponsored at the elementary school.

And I'd nearly missed this amazing opportunity, not only this particular moment, but the connections with incredible people I wouldn't have made otherwise. I'll admit I didn't participate in spouse clubs until many years into my husband's career because of some misperceptions, and only then because of an invitation from another spouse. I'm not sure I would have ever ventured forth on my own. In my younger years, I'd often heard statements like these when the topic of military spouse groups came up:

"It's too political."

"Those women are catty."

"They're so cliquish."

"I'll never be one of *those* spouses."

"They all wear their spouse's rank."

Some military spouses are of the opinion that spouse groups are relics of the past, that they're all about gossip and garden parties, things that that don't resonate with our busy, modern-day lives. I agree, the thought of women sipping tea while wearing long white gloves, discussing their husband's ranks or what the Joneses are doing doesn't appeal. Thankfully, if that was ever an accurate picture of spouse clubs—and I doubt it—the spouse groups I've been part of were far from that.

When we were stationed in Hawaii, my young friend Rose confided to me through tears that the spouse group had "literally saved my life." A brand-new spouse, she and her Navy husband arrived on the island and as often happens, he'd immediately left for a long deployment at sea. Left behind in a seemingly idyllic tropical location, she struggled not only with the newness of military life but with severe postpartum depression, sleepless nights caring for an infant, and the isolation of not knowing anyone.

"I didn't feel like I had the right to be so unhappy, living in Hawaii," she said, "but I didn't know how to help myself."

Thankfully, her neighbor in military housing, an older spouse, reached out. She connected Rose with resources for deployed spouses, counseling, and medical help. She also brought her to the spouse club. There, Rose found friends in similar circumstances. By the time I arrived, her infant was a toddler, and Rose was deeply involved with playgroups and a "brunch bunch" of young moms who met weekly. In fact, she served as a greeter at our monthly meetings and was one of the first people I met in the group. She'd come a long way from her first lonely days as a military spouse.

Rose's story is not uncommon. Yes, there are many good online resources for military spouses and ways to connect via social media, but there is simply no replacement for meeting people face to face. Enter spouse clubs! They offer playgroups, book clubs, volunteer opportunities, and so many other activities from hiking groups to foodie clubs. These organizations are also first in line to provide real support and help to deployed spouses, families with new babies, or those experiencing illness or bereavement. They often spring into action like a well-oiled machine in those circumstances, simply because their members have been-there done-that many times.

"Back in the day," as they say, officer and enlisted spouse groups were separate. Fortunately, common sense took hold and combined spouse clubs became the norm. Separate clubs exist at some locations, but they often cooperate in many ways. Regardless of rank, the military spouse experience has so many commonalities. If your spouse is deployed, you cry the same tears and feel the same fear. If you're brand new at an assignment, the loneliness doesn't differ by pay grade.

For me, getting involved with local military spouse groups, volunteering, and being part of the community was a rewarding aspect of military life. When I was starting out, I didn't expect to be one of those spouses extolling the virtues of the spouse club. However, as our family logged more deployments and moves, I discovered a growing passion to connect with and support other families going through the same experiences, especially younger or inexperienced spouses. I never wanted anyone else to feel as alone as I did as a new military spouse.

MENTORSHIP: WE CAN DO IT!

Rosie the Riveter is the iconic symbol of the women who kept things going on the home front during World War II. The picture of Rosie, sleeves rolled up, bicep flexed and ready for hard work, was part of a campaign to recruit women into defense industries and support the war effort. She quickly became a picture of strength, courage, and independence.

Rosie and the military wives of that era can seem larger than life to us modern day military spouses, but we can identify with the "We Can Do It!" spirit Rosie symbolized. My own grandmother, Mary Virginia Brown, was one of those young military wives, and I was always intrigued to hear her stories of holding down the fort while my grandfather served with the Army in Europe during World War II. She juggled life alone as she gave birth to their first child, my dad, took college classes, and worked in a telegraph office. She had no idea she wouldn't see her husband again for eighteen months. But when she talked about that time in her life, it was clear she never felt sorry for herself. She did what she felt needed to be done to help the U.S. and Allies win the war.

It is inspiring and affirming to hear stories from military spouses who have been where we're headed. And we can share our stories with those who are headed where we've been. Military life is equal parts challenging and rewarding, and every military spouse will need help at some point, the support of friends, or a strong mentor to help light the way forward.

When seasoned spouses share our experiences and sympathize with what newer military spouses are going through, we can inspire them to believe they can face whatever military life throws at them.

Terri, a veteran spouse, told me how she came to understand the importance of friendship and mentoring during her first overseas move.

"Moving to Germany was the first time I really realized how much I needed the military family," said Terri. "You know, I thought we were going on this wild vacation, but the first six months of our time there I was probably in a depression. I just couldn't believe how long it took to start feeling normal."

Terri ventured out with her small children to a playgroup at the military community center and met other young moms. She connected with them, and they became fast friends. She joined the spouse club and before long was asked to serve as president of the organization. Though she felt unqualified, Terri agreed. An older spouse saw that she was overwhelmed with her new responsibilities and gave her some welcome advice.

"Meg saw me kind of floundering. She saw me trying to please everybody, and that's a problem I have is being a major people pleaser," Terri said. "Some pretty strong voices were telling me all the different things they thought we should do as a spouse group. Meg said to me one day, 'Terri, here's something you need to build into your responses when somebody comes to you and says, 'This is a great idea.' You can say, 'Thank you for your input. I'll consider that and I'll get back to you.' You never have to make a decision right away. And then give yourself some time to decide."

Terri did find her voice. And over the coming decades of military life and as her husband, Jim, moved into more senior leadership roles, she also moved into a mentoring role.

"There began to be times when I could see somebody organically looking to me, asking me a lot of questions. I think sometimes younger people are afraid to ask somebody older, 'Will you be my mentor?' That just feels really formal, so I have often said, 'Hey, would you like to get together more regularly and just talk over coffee?' That's kind of how those things have been birthed, and they've been really good seasons of life. We get together for coffee, and I just ask how things are going and then talk through things that are important to them."

Terri offers this about being on both sides of mentorship: "During the moment you may realize, this is really somebody I can look up to. But sometimes it's not until later you look back and go yes, that person really did shape my outlook. If you're an older spouse, you may hesitate to offer advice, because we don't want to be perceived as pushy. But if you're younger and see somebody that you admire, ask them if they'd be interested in getting together with you. But manage expectations. If you get bold enough to step out and ask somebody and for whatever reason . . . they decline. Try not to get your feelings hurt or take it personally. Just understand that we're all at different places in life, and it just might not have been a good season for them. But don't let that stop you from trying again! I've had people say to me, 'Well, I'm scared to ask anybody to be my mentor—whether formally or informally—because what if they say no?' And to that I say, 'Well, what if they do say no? It's okay. Just keep looking for the next person. They weren't the right fit for you.'"

Who do you look up to? How do you find someone who can help you navigate the nuances of the military world, answer questions, explain the plethora of acronyms, or simply offer kindness and support? Finding a trusted mentor can be so important. And then, as you become more experienced, you can pass on that knowledge and be a mentor to someone else.

Mentoring is something military spouses seem to do pretty well, whether formally or informally. Most of us remember being that floundering young spouse and want to shine some light on the path for someone else. Our hope is to let them know what they're feeling isn't strange and that they don't need to navigate military life alone. To remind them how strong they really are.

A THOUSAND TIMES OVER

Chelsea Davis is one of the founders of *The Submerged Life* blog for submarine spouses and families around the world. When she met her Navy man, the only thing she was certain about was that she was in love. Until that point, she hadn't ever imagined being a military wife.

"I grew up in Washington state in a Navy town," said Chelsea. "My family wasn't affiliated with the military at all, but all my childhood friends had parents in the Navy. And I kind of took the stance of, *I'm never going to marry in the Navy. I'm never gonna date a guy in the Navy. I'm never going to be a military spouse.* I went off to college to study journalism and public relations in Seattle and, lo and behold, I met my now husband who was a submariner. But while we were dating, I lived and worked in Seattle, and I wasn't privy to his Navy life. He was more of a weekend boyfriend. He'd go out to sea for weeks or a few months at a time, and I was living my best life with my college girlfriends in an apartment, doing my thing and working. We did a long-distance year, and he went to Bahrain, and then eventually we moved to California and got married."

Moving away from her home state, settling into a new place, then spending months alone during deployment forced Chelsea to come to terms quickly with what it meant to love someone on active duty. She soon realized the only way to make it work was to come to a place of acceptance.

"A lot of people say to me, 'Chelsea, I don't know how you do it; I could *never* do what you do.' I really hate that statement, though it comes from such a good place. But I just say to them, 'Just imagine the person you love. This is their job, this is their passion, this is their calling. They chose to serve their country. This is what they do—something bigger than them. And it comes with these sacrifices. You don't know how I do it? I do it because I love him. It's that simple.'"

Though Chelsea comes across as positive, informed, and cheerful, her initial transition to military life was something of a shock.

"I had no idea what I was doing and had no handbook, no guidebook to this crazy life—all the acronyms and the way of life."

Though she thought they'd be settled in California for some time, as often happens, Chelsea's husband received orders to Naval Submarine Base New London in Connecticut. James was scheduled to be there for six months. So, they packed up their car and got ready to move across country.

"We had all of our life in that car. Us and our corgi, driving off into the sunset," said Chelsea. Then came the call. James's orders had been changed. To Guam.

"I had a massive meltdown in the car," Chelsea remembers. "I was just so confused and overwhelmed. We'd just gotten married. I'm working. I can't point Guam out on a map, and I don't know anything about it, but I'm very Type A and get into problem solving mode. And I'm like, *okay, I'm gonna start Googling; we're gonna figure this out.* Guam had a really great tourism website, i.e., 'Come visit Guam,' but nothing about picking up your life and moving there."

The lack of information and discovering the remoteness of the island, in Chelsea's words, "freaked me out." As often happens in military life, four days later the orders were changed again. Back to Connecticut. Chelsea was getting a crash course in the flexibility required by military life.

"I learned the hard way that verbal orders don't really mean anything until it's in writing. So, I had all that meltdown for no reason."

The couple were stationed in Connecticut for three years, where they welcomed their first child. Chelsea's early experience of desperately looking for information about an upcoming PCS stayed with her.

"As a Navy wife, I just needed a one-stop shop where I could get some answers to my questions, my fears, you know, silly things like, 'Does Amazon ship there?' All the little mundane things that add up to your normal life. And I just kept thinking, I can't be the only one who gets so overwhelmed and needs answers. And you know, I love my husband, but they can only help so much. And so that led me to think, what if there was an online resource specifically for submarine duty stations?"

In 2019, Chelsea and two other submarine spouses, Meagan Guise and Kaileigh Lear, joined forces to create *The Submerged Life*. With guest writers and contributors from submarine bases across the U.S. and overseas, they've created the resource Chelsea longed for as a new Navy spouse. Along with providing help for other military families and connecting with her fellow submarine spouses, Chelsea has also found her own confidence to face military life realistically.

"This life is not easy. It can be very emotional, very stressful. But I could sit here and think of all the reasons to feel sorry for myself: It's so hard to move every two to three years. It's hard being away from friends and family. It's hard finding someone who would hire me as a military spouse. My husband was out to sea nine months this year. I could go on and on, but I think it's okay to feel salty. Give yourself space to feel it, allow yourself to sit in those feelings, but I always have to come out of it because this is my life. I love my husband, I chose my husband, and I would do it a thousand times over."

FRIENDS INDEED

When I met Lana, she was the president of the spouse club at our assignment in Hawaii. In that position, Lana coordinated numerous base-wide events and volunteer efforts. As I volunteered alongside her over the next couple of years, I learned more about her and how difficult the adjustment to being a military spouse had been for her.

After marrying her Air Force husband, having a baby, and moving overseas, Lana found herself derailed from pursuing her master's degree and unable to follow the career path she'd always envisioned. Instead, she was a brand-new mom to an infant with his own idea of what was important—namely, feeding and diaper changes—and a military spouse newly arrived in Germany. This was not what she'd imagined her life would be as a first-time mother.

"I came from a large extended family, and people were there to help when you had a baby. Grandma or Auntie would watch your kid while you went to the store. Since we were overseas, we didn't have that. But when I had my first child, I thought, *I can do this. I don't need help!*"

She and her husband, Maurice, found connections difficult in military housing where they lived.

"I was in my mid-twenties, and it seemed like the community we moved into always wanted to go out and party. That was not my jam. I just wanted to be quiet and alone with my baby. But I was really lonely. I was adjusting to a new country. I couldn't find women that had my same interests. Looking back, I can see that was my own fault. I kept everyone at arm's length. And I did that for four years. I'm a slow learner!"

After the military moved them to Hawaii, Lana was determined to approach things differently. She joined some spouse groups, began reaching out more, and made peace with the uncomfortable thought that rejection was a possibility.

"I kept trying to reach out, and finally meeting a few people I felt comfortable with helped," she said. "But when I find my people, it's hard for me to move on. And the military doesn't really allow for that. You *will* move on."

In spite of the inevitable goodbyes, Lana found that making meaningful connections made military life so much easier.

"I wish I could go back and tell my younger self, 'Get over yourself. You're not going to like a lot of people. Deal with it! You're not always the most pleasant person to be with, either,'" she said. "I wish I hadn't wasted four years. One thing I learned was that you must give people grace; also, that expectations have always gotten me into trouble. Whatever you think—how your children will be, what your marriage looks like—I think you should work toward something, but not be invested in how it turns out because you can't control the outcome."

Stacy has also learned the importance of friendship. She's the mom to a "magnificent Marine" son and two teenage daughters, and now a grandmother. She's also a military veteran herself and a longtime Army spouse.

After serving in the Air Force for fourteen years, Stacy suffered a stroke that ended her military career. Suddenly, she was "just" a military spouse and found it difficult to navigate that new world outside of life on active duty.

"Military life for spouses is a lonely life. It really is if you don't have a true tribe," she said. "And when we lived in Texas, I didn't have a tribe at first. At my loneliest point, I decided to just go out and start meeting people and not be a hermit. And I was still trying to adjust from leaving the military. I didn't know how to communicate with people unless we were 'talking shop.' So, I had to learn."

Stacy experienced the support of the military community as the mother of a service member. When Hurricane Florence swept through Marine Corps Base Camp Lejeune,

North Carolina, in 2018, it upended the wedding plans of her Marine Corps son, Jordan, and his fiancée, Jillia. The disaster flooded the prospective wedding venue in North Carolina and affected Jordan's training dates, pushing them forward. He and Jillia wanted to marry before he left for training, so they decided to get married in Texas, where Jillia was living. Since they made the decision one day and got married the next, Stacy and her husband could not get there in time. To help make the wedding day special, Stacy reached out to military spouse friends who were living in Texas.

"They said, 'We've got you. Don't worry about it.'" said Stacy. "My friend Theresa put out an all-points bulletin asking for help."

Within hours, military spouses had arranged a photographer, wedding cake, and decorations for the impromptu event. The network of military moms in Texas came in and surrounded Jordan and Jillia with love, care, and all the trimmings for a wedding, reception, and even honeymoon.

This story is unique, but not rare. Military spouses have a long history of supporting one another. Over time, Stacy realized that being open to friendships she wouldn't have normally pursued in the past ended up changing her life for the better.

FRIENDS OLD AND NEW

One of the conversations I had at Bob Hope Village was with Anita, Donna, and Mary, a group of Vietnam-era spouses, now widowed. They told me about friendships past and present and how those relationships make military life joyful, even in hard times.

Anita grew up in England, met her American Air Force husband in 1957 and came to the United States in 1960. After they moved to California, her husband would do two Vietnam tours. The coming years would be a challenge for the family.

"By then, we had four small children. It was very hard. Dreadful, actually."

But Anita said friendships made the time bearable.

"It helps that we had an Air Force family. Nobody else understands what you did without, what you went through, what you had to do by yourself . . ." Anita's voice trailed off as she remembered, but then she brightened.

"But you just get up and cope. What choice do you have? You meet such wonderful people. I mean, there are oddballs once in a while, of course. And we moved three times in one year! It was one thing after another. But if you've got common sense, you can do anything. I mean, you might not do it *right*, but still."

Donna met her husband, an Air Force medic, in her Louisiana hometown. She had never lived anywhere else until she got married and moved to Topeka, Kansas. For her, it was nearly as big a culture shock as if she'd moved overseas, and her Southern accent created a language barrier.

"No one could understand me!" she exclaimed. "I'd take a book and go in front of the bathroom mirror, read the book out loud and watch my mouth. I wanted to get rid of that accent—I was tired of people saying, 'Well, honey, where are you from and why are you here?'"

Donna also faced the difficulties of raising kids alone while her husband served overseas or was away for temporary duty assignments.

"We weren't married too long, and he was off to Vietnam," she said. "He was gone eighty-nine days out of every ninety for five years. No relatives within a thousand miles on either side, so it's a good thing I had good neighbors. I mean, if your child gets sick, what do you do with the others?"

She spoke about the challenge and the need for finding friends after a move.

"You have to just reach and touch your neighbors and make friends. You just have to. Most of our moves, we'd land in an empty house, and my husband would go off to training or overseas. Who do you think did it all?"

Mary joined the Air Force in 1965, though she later left the service to marry a fellow Airman. Her husband spent nearly eight years going back and forth to Vietnam while the family lived overseas. They lived in locations like Okinawa and England, and Mary embraced military life.

"I loved moving. Always seeing something new—I loved it," she said. "I liked knowing if you didn't like your neighbors, someone was moving on. I didn't like settling down at all when my husband retired."

After going through her husband's years-long battle with Alzheimer's, she said she knew she'd wind up at Bob Hope Village one day.

"It's just like being back in a military community," she said, adding that she loves hearing the planes flying overhead from nearby Eglin AFB.

Mary said life at Bob Hope is not unlike her younger days as a military spouse.

"The more you got into your community, the better it was. I liked everywhere we lived because I got involved. And being here now, there's something to do every day. If you're not involved, it's your own fault! We look out for each other, just like we did when we were younger."

Not that it's been easy, this transition from military spouse, to retirement, to widowhood.

"I've learned to re-find myself. It's been a good experience. For the first time after fifty years, I'm learning who I am. After my husband died, I knew, no matter what I had to face in all those years, I could make it, because I know I have all the support I ever need right here. Someone will come up and tell you they're praying for you. It's not like a big church, where the only person you know is the one right beside you; it's like a big family. You know that people care."

She paused and said with a smile, "I mean, you do have those crazy cousins . . . ."

My recorded conversation with the military wives at Bob Hope village ended in peals of laughter, friends old and new, finding joy in their shared connection. Later, listening to that recording again, I wished for more time to ask those wise women all the questions that come to my mind now. *How did you do it? How did you get through the fear? How did you manage the long days of war with no news? How did you handle living in a new place alone when you didn't know anyone?*

But I suspect I have the answer already. I hear Anita's sensible voice saying, "You just get up and cope," Donna adding, "You just have to reach out and make friends," and Mary chiming in, "Look out for each other."

Faithful friends—May we know them. May we be them.

PART 5

THE REST OF
THE STORY

FORGING A NEW PATH

See, I am doing a new thing! Now it springs up;
do you not perceive it? I am making a way in the wilderness
and streams in the wasteland. —Isaiah 43:19 (NIV)

I heard my mother crying on the phone in the adjoining room.

"Oh no!" she said through her tears. "Okay, okay. I'll try to get out tomorrow."

Her father, my beloved Papaw, had been in ill health for some months, but the death of someone you love is always shocking news with its finality, its grimness. After conferring with my dad and calling the airline to reschedule her flights, she retreated to her room to pack her bags and leave our house well before she'd planned. My own heart ached at the loss of my grandfather, and I suddenly realized there was no way I'd be able to make his funeral.

I looked across the living room to where my son Matthew lay on the couch, cocooned in blankets, asleep and oblivious to our conversation, still under the effects of the anesthesia and medication from his surgery that morning. He looked vulnerable and smaller than his nine years, the way sleeping children always do. He'd had a rough time after the surgery to repair a hernia, including a bad reaction to the anesthesia. We'd only just gotten him home in the early evening and made him comfortable.

My mom had arrived at our house in Florida a few days earlier to help me with our other three children while Matthew, the oldest, underwent his needed surgery. Steve was away in the middle of a six-week TDY, and I was glad for her help. Mom had always been such a champ at times like this, coming to stay and help with the kids and household tasks, and had spent weeks with us after I gave birth to each of our four children. In fact, she'd been with me at the delivery of our second son Gabriel when Steve was away.

Of course, there was no question that she'd return home to New Mexico immediately at this devastating news. My mind raced at possible scenarios for me to get to Papaw's funeral, but I came up empty. There was simply no way I could or would leave my son with friends or another caregiver. He needed me. As torn as I felt, I knew this milestone would be added to the list of others I'd missed.

Over the years, there were so many family events—both happy and sad—that, as a young woman, I'd never dreamed of missing. I would have protested, *absolutely no way*. My grandparents had all been close to me my entire life. I would never have chosen to miss any of their funerals, but I missed two of them due to situations like Matthew's surgery, the logistics of living overseas, and/or Steve being away on military service. There were so many moments I'd long to be "back home" or wish I could attend a happy event like a wedding or family reunion. I missed my youngest brother's wedding while we were stationed in Guam. Often, I had to decline because of the prohibitive cost of flying a family of six stateside from overseas; or my desire not to leave and be half the world away from small children for whom I was the primary caretaker.

These were not easy choices. At one family gathering I was actually able to attend now that we're retired and live closer to family, someone made a flippant remark about us "choosing not to come" to certain events over the past years.

I bit back an acid retort—because lashing out would be fruitless. How could I explain the angst we went through over missing milestones and events, the tears I'd shed over about being so far away, the longing to stay connected, the difficult decisions we were forced to make. Anyone who would make such an unfeeling remark probably wouldn't understand, anyway. (And hey—roads and planes go both ways, last I checked.)

SHOULD I STAY, OR SHOULD I GO?

The decision whether to go or stay in a military career often comes up around the decade point. For us, this meant half-way to retirement, as Steve was eligible for retirement at twenty years. And when we weighed all the pros and cons—despite all the missing out and sacrifices—it made sense for him to stay in the Air Force, as we were already halfway there.

But as he approached his twenty-year mark, he surprised me by considering continuing his military service beyond that point. It was not something I'd really thought about. The demarcation of twenty years seemed like a finish line, a "we did it!" feeling. It would mean we could get back to "normal" life, live closer to family and not miss out on so much. But, as with many military members, he still had opportunities for advancement at that point.

The effect of military life on our kids was not lost on us, of course. When Steve hit the "Do I stay, or do I go?" decision phase of his military career, our older children were teenagers and all they'd known was military life. We discussed it with them, and they, too, wanted to continue the adventure, and so onward we went. When we made the decision that Steve would continue his service, I had no idea it would mean another eleven years of Air Force life!

As you continue with long-term military service, your circle gets smaller and you start to see the same people repeatedly, which can be both bad and good, of course. Coveted job opportunities get competitive, and if you're continuing to move up, it may also mean that the moves increase. During one span of six years, we moved every single year for new assignments or mandated moves to different military housing. This was also the era in which I found myself standing at the gas pump racking my brain for my latest zip code.

While it can be tempting to look at those years only through the lens of sacrifice, I'm also reminded of the memories we made during those final eleven years. Each of our sons met their future wives at a place the military sent us. Grace discovered her passion for art, and developed her talent through classes, visiting art museums, and taking photos of beautiful landscapes in Washington, DC, and Europe. Anna fell in love with Irish dance in a class at an on-base youth center. She persevered with her craft through moves and different dance schools, eventually landing in an incredible school where we retired in Texas. She's now a world ranked dancer and is still traveling the world.

Together, we experienced the beauty and diversity and excitement of living in places like Germany and Hawaii. I connected with a second career, landed a remote job that I was able to take with me on our last few moves, and found a new passion for writing and editing. We made incredible friends, created memories, and traveled together.

Was it worth missing all the events, experiencing the distance from extended family, sacrificing so many moments we'd never get back? Was it? This question is not easily distilled into an either/or conclusion. There's no way to know what our path would have looked like had Steve chosen to get out of the military sooner. All I know is the hand we were dealt.

And most days, I come to the conclusion that it was pretty good.

THE LAST PARADE

Let the bugle blow
Let the march be played
With the forming of the troops
For my last parade.

The years of war and the years of waiting
Obedience to orders, unhesitating
Years in the States, and the years overseas
All woven in a web of memories.

A lifetime of service passes in review
As many good friends and exotic places too
In the waning sunlight begin to fade
With the martial music of my last parade.

My last salute to the service and base
Now someone else will take my place
To the sharp young airmen marching away
I gladly pass the orders of the day.

Though uncertain of what my future may hold
Still, if needed— before I grow too old
I'll keep my saber sharp, my powder dry
Lest I be recalled to duty by and by.

So let the bugle blow
Fire the evening gun
Slowly lower the colors
My retirement has begun.
—Author Unknown, "The Last Parade"

At the end of a long military career, you know the end is coming—it's inevitable. Still, after all those years, military life has become part of who you are, not just for the servicemember, but for the family, too.

As we faced Steve's upcoming retirement ceremony and what our life would be like when the military no longer defined what we did and how we lived, we began the proverbial walk down memory lane. You can't help but take stock of how you've spent your life over that many years.

We've been through a lot together: getting married when he was a baby Airman and I a young nursing school student, having babies far from extended family, living overseas, years spent apart during deployments and military mandated separations, moving when the kids were little, moving when they were big, eighteen homes, that one time we went through two typhoons in one week, travel to amazing places, and so much more. During his military service, Steve traveled to six of the seven continents, including Antarctica—twice. (By the way, I think we need to hit South America and mark that off your list, dear!) How can you even begin to put the tapestry of experiences and memories into words?

At his retirement ceremony, I watched Steve at the head of the ballroom. After the busyness of planning the events and the dinner preceding this final moment, surrounded by friends and family who'd flown in for the event, it all came down to this final goodbye to the military. He was still tall and handsome, impressive in his dress blues, chest covered with ribbons and medals.

My mind flashed back to that young Airman he once was, with only a couple of stripes on his sleeve. I loved him now even more than I did then. He looked too young to have served three decades—everyone said it—but the memories, tears, and years behind us told us otherwise. I beamed with pride as I watched him go through the formalities, receive and give his final salute, accept the folded flag. *Well done*, I thought.

During part of the presentation, as photos of our family through the years flickered on the overhead screen, our song "Would You Go with Me?" was part of the background music track. It was all I could do not to turn into a blubbering mess right then, as the music played and I gazed at the slideshow, watching our family morph from just Steve and me as young-sters to a young bustling family with lots of littles, to now parents of young adults, and of all things, grandparents. It had all happened so quickly. And when Steve made a point to thank our children for their years of sacrifice and flexibility and then called me up to recognize me and give me a gift, I felt humbled. One of his gifts to me was an Apple Watch, he said, as a "symbol of all the time I want to give back to you." We smiled at each other through tears, understanding how many moments big and small we'd missed together.

As we faced this latest transition in the long line of what have been years of living in transition, there was some famil-iarity, but also new, unexpected moments. I said often in the lead-up to the final ceremony that military retirement is hard to describe, but there are three other events I can compare it to: graduation, marriage, and a memorial service.

It's like a graduation, because everyone keeps saying, *You made it!*

We know we're moving on to the coveted next step: the greener grass of life after the military. There's a lot behind us, and hopefully we're a bit smarter than when we first started this journey.

Also: You get presents!

It's like a wedding, because it's the start of a new life. Also: logistics, logistics, logistics. Picking out venues and menus and going through years of photos for the ceremony slideshow. (If you're planning to do this, go through your photos well ahead of time. It took me so much longer than I'd expected!) We had to figure out where guests would stay and eat, line up their transportation. So many little details. Then there's all the formality: walking in with an escort, dressing up, seating, protocol rules, and a receiving line. The special moments that come with reconnecting with loved ones who make the trip for this, your special day.

The flurry of details will threaten to overshadow the importance of what's happening, just like pre-wedding planning does. I had to take a moment to step back and make time to process my own thoughts and feelings.

Also: You get presents!

It's like a memorial service, because it marks the end of a chapter, of a way of life. It may seem silly to say that a military retirement ceremony seems like a memorial service, considering we were present for it. But it is surreal in so many ways to watch the sunset of your spouse's military career. Steve's military service was something that had defined him, had been an integral part of who he was for as long as I'd known him.

When the somber commands "Publish the order," and "You are relieved from active duty," were spoken, the finality hit me: *It's over.*

He was finished. Someone else would take care of his airmen and "his Air Force." It was time to pass the responsibility on and let go.

One reason ceremonies are so appealing is that they give us the final retrospective. Closure. The chance to mull over all that's come before, decisions made, the people who changed us. To mark a moment in time where you say *farewell* while you look forward and feel satisfaction in a job well done.

These are the final words my husband spoke from 2 Timothy 4:7-8 at the end of his retirement ceremony:

I have fought the good fight, I have finished the race, I have kept the faith.

And to that, I say, *well done, babe.*

A NEW NORMAL

In the time leading up to Steve's retirement from the Air Force, I did my best to prepare like I do for any major life event. I rotated between devouring the bajillion pamphlets the military dispenses on cheerful topics like "Why you should sign up for the Survivor Benefits Plan" and the eleventy-seven steps your spouse needs to complete to maybe, possibly, receive VA benefits. I Googled helpful phrases like "What the frick do I do now after being a military spouse for three decades?" and munched chocolate while staring out the window of our ancient base house and tried to imagine what life would be like after years of living in houses just like this.

Pretty sure that last activity was easily as helpful as any other "preparation" I could manage.

Still, we treated this final transition almost like a typical PCS move, which is helpful in some ways, except for the fact that it's *not* a PCS. Or typical. The reality of this hit home when, after the rush of goodbyes, gifts, and well wishes, we left our last base in Virginia, rolled into our new neighborhood in Texas, and met—*crickets.* No one was there to meet us, introduce us to the area, or even give a flip that we were here. There was no newcomers' orientation, no friendly neighbor asking if I wanted to join the spouse club. No one was there to make Steve's way smooth as he jumped right into his next military job, because there wasn't one.

If you're a long-time military spouse facing or going through retirement, your experience may not be just like mine. But now, after gaining the distance of a few years from active military life and comparing notes with other spouses, I've got a little perspective, especially about the big surprises of life after active-duty service. Here are a few things I've noticed.

How much military life defined mine: My friend Lana, who we met earlier, noted on an Instagram post I made after Steve retired that her husband's retirement felt like "I almost lit a match to the last twenty-plus years of my life."

This!

While I'd taken care to craft my own identity, I, too, hadn't realized how much what I did revolved around the military. Military life provided me instant friends, gave me instant activities, and made things fairly easy in the social realm. Now there was a void I would have to intentionally fill.

How exhausted I was: The last ten or fifteen years of Steve's career had been fast moving—a new assignment every two years or less, including multiple overseas and back from overseas moves, constant TDYs on his part, and long deployments. *I. Was. Spent.* When that stress was lifted, I felt run over. I slept a lot during the first weeks.

The relief: Along with the exhaustion, a weight fell off, a heavy load I didn't even realize I was carrying, as I'd borne it for so many years without questioning it. I won't ever have to wave goodbye again as my husband ships out to a dangerous place, tear a child away from all they've known for the past few years, or restart a career because of a move. *Wow.*

Feeling disconnected: Though our oldest son was himself serving in the Air Force at the time of Steve's retirement, and I continue to work for a military-oriented company and write for military publications, the sense of disconnect from the military spouse community was something I didn't foresee. They'd been part of my life for so long.

I needed to make space for my husband: Even after over thirty years, our marriage is still and always a work in progress. We'd both become so accustomed to being apart regularly, that when we were suddenly together all the time, it took some effort to readjust. For my part, I needed to welcome him back into decision-making and not resent his input on everyday decisions I'd made alone for years. I reminded myself to be thankful that he was here, and that I had someone to rely on again, a partner. I was so accustomed to figuring everything out myself and filling him in later, and I needed to remember to make room for us.

My reaction to the word *forever:* As we shopped for a home to buy, I can't tell you how many times a well-meaning person said to me, "Aren't you so excited to find your *forever home?*" These words made me want to flee. *Forever?* I wasn't prepared to make that sort of commitment after years of temporary quarters and military housing. When we decided we would stay in the house for five years (still a long time) and then reassess, the pressure lifted.

How long it would take for my husband to find a second career: I had visions of executives knocking down his door before Steve even left active duty. Of *course*, they'd wish to take advantage of his well-honed skills and education. Instead, it took some months for him to land the right job. While he savored the time puttering around the new house and repainting the deck, I had moments of panic. At one point he reminded me gently, "God's always taken care of us before. Why would He stop now?"

Changes in relationships: Knowing that a friendship will require long-term work on my part is a new concept, too. Apparently, I have sweepingly wide commitment issues I didn't foresee. I'm more cautious about jumping right in the way I used to, which seems silly after all my years of preaching, "Bloom where you're planted." But I'm aware of it and working on it.

Difficulty making decisions: From choosing a church, to where we should live, to hanging up pictures, every decision feels weightier. I have a surprisingly hard time making decisions, though I'm naturally assertive and usually know what I want. My upstairs loft is still not decorated!

Permanence: When I place a box of Christmas ornaments on a shelf, I don't have to worry about whether it's packed well enough to make it through the next unexpected move, because it will be *on that same shelf next Christmas season*, unless I move it. When I say goodbye to the hairdresser or dentist after an appointment, I don't have to count down how many more times I'll see them. If I choose, I can keep coming back for years. This is weird, while also comforting. And I think, *Is this how people live? Is this how I used to live before I got married?* I've forgotten.

What I miss: Little things, really, like hearing "Taps" at bedtime or the national anthem at the end of the duty day. Running around the corner to the commissary or the small town feel of living on a military base. Our first night sleeping in the house we bought was strange and even a little frightening. We'd lived in the equivalent of a gated, guarded community for so many years in military housing.

How much I *don't* miss: This is perhaps most surprising of all. I truly thought I might pine away for *what was*. I haven't, really, after the initial shock of civilian life. I don't miss the fishbowl existence I felt during Steve's last years of service or a calendar constantly filled with events not always of my choosing. I thought I'd miss it more. Maybe I will someday, but for now, I'm enjoying the more laid-back lifestyle of working from home and going out when I feel like it.

As we face the coming years of life after the military, I'm sure there will be even more I realize I miss—or not. Military spouse life will always make up part of the fabric of who I am.

But looking forward, *I'm excited!*

NOT QUITE CINDERELLA

Steve and I were still a young dating couple when I attended my first military function. I had no idea what to expect. No concept of military protocol, no idea what rank insignia or a service dress coat filled with ribbons and medals signified. As we walked into the event, I nervously smoothed the front of the emerald satin floor-length gown I'd borrowed from a friend.

"You look beautiful," Steve whispered into my ear. "Don't worry."

Steve had been chosen as Airman of the Quarter at his workplace and was then nominated for the installation's Airman of the Year award, which would be announced at that event. In my naivete, I was certain this was all a formality and that of course he'd win. He was awesome, after all.

We entered the officers club ballroom, festooned with flags, its long linen-draped tables adorned with giant floral centerpieces, crystal, and silver. Steve introduced me to his supervisors and commanders. All the stripes and brass on their uniforms told me these people were important, but it made as much sense to me as trying to read Latin. To my mind, I was sure they were honored to talk to him, the certain winner of Airman of the Year.

I watched as other military wives and significant others floated around the room in their beautiful ball gowns, seemingly comfortable and in their element, but they talked to each other and not to me. After the playing of the national anthem, which brought unexpected tears to my eyes, and the chaplain's invocation, we were seated.

Before the food was served, we were instructed to observe some moments of silence by the ceremony's emcee. He directed us to take note of a small square table at the front of the ballroom. It was covered with a white linen tablecloth like the other banquet tables, but it had a different place setting and a chair leaned against it. I listened with interest as he explained that it was the POW/MIA table, there to honor and remember American prisoners of war and those missing in action. Each item on the table was full of meaning: a single red rose to represent life and bloodshed, salt to signify tears, a slice of lemon to remind us of their bitter fate, an inverted glass to denote their inability to be present with us, and a chair tilted against the table. He informed us that a tilted chair will remain at every military event for those who cannot be there *until they all come home.* At the time, I hadn't realized there were still military members missing in action around the world. After the solemnity of those moments, I tucked away all I had learned to mull over later.

When I turned my attention to my own place setting, I discovered more knives and forks than I knew what to do with. I quietly observed others at our table to see which piece of cutlery to use when. As the evening went on and I relaxed a little, I watched in fascination as active-duty members were sent to the "grog bowl" for various infractions of manners or protocol.

This particular event was a "dining out," which in the Air Force is a formal military dinner with very specific procedures called "rules of the mess." Other service branches have similar events, all rooted in similar military history. I didn't know any of this at this first event. I was just fascinated by the spectacle.

A grog bowl is a specific feature of a dining out—as well as a "dining in," a similar event that does not include spouses and significant others. The grog bowl is a giant punchbowl, sometimes even an unused toilet bowl, filled with whatever booze is handy and anything else military folks want to throw in: Tabasco sauce, salt, coffee, candy, anything random they could find—even socks. These events usually include a non-alcoholic and equally icky version for non-drinkers and designated drivers. The military-focused publication *We Are the Mighty* gives the concoction a fitting description: "the bottom-dwelling juices of a trash compactor."[1]

That night it was absolutely gross, this roiling brown version of punch, and it served the purpose of punishment for infractions of the "rules of the mess"—real or imagined—such as picking up their fork before the head of the table or leaving to go to the restroom. It was all good-natured fun, and commanders and airmen alike made the reluctant march to the grog bowl over the course of the evening for made-up infractions. They'd force down a cup of the nasty brew and hold the empty glass upside down over their heads to cheers across the hall.

Watching the frequent treks to the grog bowl and the constant teasing that went on between the military members, I was surprised by the atmosphere. Steve said the event was a formal one, so I'd expected a restrained, quiet, even boring gathering. The only military events or settings I'd seen up to that point had been on TV or in movies. This event wasn't like any of that, and it was anything but restrained. I was amused by the strange contrast of the cursing, drinking, joking, and familiarity juxtaposed with the somber moments, formal gowns, military dress uniforms, giant flower arrangements, glittering china and crystal, and the gourmet dinner we were served.

Steve did win Airman of the Year that night, as I knew he would. We proudly posed for photos after the ceremony and headed home. *Done and dusted,* I thought. I couldn't imagine I would have a chance to attend another event like that anytime soon—or ever. Little did I know.

After Steve and I were married and his career continued, formal dinners, yearly balls, ceremonies for promotions, retirements, and changes of command became a regular part of our lives. Like many long-time military wives, I ended up with a closet full of ball gowns and "little black dresses" that I regularly rotated, changing out jewelry and accessories for different looks.

Some afternoons I'd get a text from Steve saying, "Remember we have that dinner tonight?" and often the answer was "No, I did not remember," but I would drop what I was doing and hurriedly get ready. Quite a change from the nerves and careful wardrobe planning of my first few years as a military girlfriend and wife. One thing hasn't changed: I still tear up when I hear "The Star-Spangled Banner" playing, no matter how many times I hear it.

And like the servicemembers I'd observed at that first military awards banquet, I've also learned not to take myself too seriously. Certainly, one trait that helped with that was my innate klutziness. At one event, I tripped over the threshold as we entered a holiday gathering at the home of the commanding general. There was a receiving line, and after my stumble I managed to regain my balance right in front of the general, where he and his wife stood ready to welcome us. I stood upright, threw my hands into the air like a gymnast sticking the landing, and exclaimed, "Ta-da!" Thankfully, they had a sense of humor and laughed with me.

More than once I've attempted to remain stoic on the front row during a long-winded speech, as my carefully-anchored Spanx slowly and maliciously rolled down to a spot where rescue was impossible without an awkward scene. I've ripped a hole in my black opaque tights right before walking into an event, and once I knocked over my glass of water at the head table when Steve was the guest speaker. I could go on, but that's enough humility for one day.

After Steve had been retired from the military for a couple of years, I finally went through the collection of gowns and black cocktail dresses that were now gathering dust at the back of my closet. I'd held onto them long enough "just in case," but there hadn't been a case requiring them so far in my new civilian life.

I decided it was time to donate them to a nearby spouse club thrift shop. As I folded each one and placed it in the box, the memories replayed. I *wore this one to the last change of command we attended; this one to Steve's retirement dinner, this one to the Key Spouse of the Year awards, this one to our last-ever Air Force ball.* And I smiled as I remembered those moments.

I thought about the people I'd connected with through the years, so many wonderful people. I reminisced about the behind-the-scenes moments no one else saw: holding hands with Steve under the tablecloth while we watched a too-long awards ceremony; holding up my long skirt and tottering in high heels across a rainy parking lot because we were late; Steve asking me to somehow stuff his car keys into my tiny clutch purse already crammed with feminine products and lipstick; bickering in the car on the way to an event and then pasting on smiles to get through the evening until we could finish the argument later. (If you haven't been there for this one, I think you're either fibbing or just haven't hit that point in your relationship yet.)

I thought about all the ceremonies and events we'd attended together, the joyful promotions, meaningful awards and retirements, and heartbreaking funerals. Not only had I made the journey from being a young, inexperienced girlfriend to a longtime seasoned military spouse, I'd made a lot of unforgettable memories in the process. I'd learned so much, not just about military life, but about people and about the world. This military journey has given me more gifts than I realized.

I've come a long way since that first borrowed emerald-green dress.

CONCLUSION:
A NOTE TO MY YOUNGER SELF

Other than the tight bod and unwrinkled skin, I wouldn't trade places with twenty-year-old me. The hard-won lessons I've learned and experiences I've had are too precious to wish to turn back the hands of time now. But if I could write a letter to the quiet, insecure girl I once was, here's what I'd tell her:

Don't worry so much about what people think. There will always be someone who will find fault with what you're doing, so go ahead and live your life. You can't please everyone, and you'd probably be a little bit boring if you could.

Keep your sense of humor. You'll need it when the washer leaks, the baby has croup, and your eight-year-old needs stitches—all on the first day of a long deployment. You'll need it on hour fourteen of a twenty-two-hour labor. The tears will come, too, but learn the art of laughing at yourself and these ridiculous situations. It will stand you in good stead and go a long way toward smoothing over the rough spots.

Embrace the new. Don't be afraid of the unknown. "Different" doesn't equal "bad." You're about to learn a lot about the world and—through that lens—about yourself. Yes, you had a great upbringing surrounded by a loving family, but don't be afraid now to step out of that bubble. You'll be okay.

You're going places. All those places you've dreamed about visiting. Yeah, you'll see Paris. And Rome and London, too. In the words of Dr. Seuss, "Oh, the places you'll go!" I swear I'm not making this up. You'll snorkel the Great Barrier Reef, live on Pacific islands, ski in the Alps, travel in Europe, and live overseas for seven years. Hang on for a great ride!

Recognize true friendship when you see it. Some of your best friends will have lives that bear no resemblance to yours. That's how you grow, and frankly if your friends were exactly like you, you'd be redundant. They will be older and younger than you, have different beliefs, but you'll be blessed to know them. Keep your heart and mind open. You'll learn quickly that rank and jobs have nothing to do with true friendship. The ones who bring you chocolate and hold your hand during deployments, drive you to the ER when you're hacking up a lung from pneumonia, watch your other little ones while you're at the hospital delivering a baby prematurely, walk with you through the dark days following miscarriage, and cry with and cling to you when you move away—those friendships will prove to be absolutely priceless.

You're stronger than you think. Yes, your marriage is your most important relationship, but you're going to discover a strength in yourself you didn't know existed. You'll survive multiple deployments, natural disasters, goodbyes, moves across the country and around the world (not to mention moves you'll handle *alone* around the world!) and—well, I have to leave some things to your imagination, don't I? You may not do it perfectly, but you'll get through it. Don't be afraid. *You can do this.*

Take care of yourself. You won't have extended family around to help you pick up the slack. You'll have to learn to pace yourself and know that you can't be everything to everyone. It will be so easy to let all the tasks you need to accomplish take over your day. Remember what your grandmother said, "You're a human *being*, not a human *doing*." So, pace yourself. Try to be as kind to yourself as you are to others. Cultivate your faith and your friendships. Give yourself permission to relax, read a book, take a walk, soak in the tub. The world will not stop turning if you rest, trust me!

Enjoy the small moments. Don't always be looking ahead, anticipating what is to come—yes, even when you're in the middle of that frigid North Dakota winter! Take time to notice what is going on around you right now. You will lose some of the most important people in your life, your children will grow up and set off on their own, and, believe me, you will wish you could go back and enjoy those small moments again.

You're on the brink of an amazing life! *Drink it in, girl.*

ACKNOWLEDGMENTS

As with any book, this one would not be possible without the support and help of so many people, including the current and veteran military spouses who candidly shared their stories with me and allowed us all a peek into what they've experienced. I'm eternally grateful!

Thank you to all the amazing military spouses and civilian friends who've marked my life through the past decades. There are so many of you that I won't try to list them for fear of leaving someone out, but *you know*. You made military spouse life so bearable, joyful, and unforgettable.

Thanks to Shari Popejoy, who believed in this vision from the beginning. I'll always remember your encouragement, kindness, and wisdom when this was only an idea.

Thanks to the Air Force Enlisted Village, Brooke McClean, and Scarlett Bauman for facilitating my talks with the wonderful widows and couples at Bob Hope Village and for all the important work you do there every day.

Thanks to fellow writer Julie Tully, who connected me with W. Brand Publishing after I sent a text asking, "What are they *really* like?"

Thanks to JuLee and W. Brand Publishing, who jumped into this project with me wholeheartedly. So glad to be on this journey with you!

Thanks to Terri Barnes, editor extraordinaire and fellow veteran milspouse. I am beyond grateful for your expertise and wisdom and your encouragement and belief in the importance of these stories. Thank you for keeping me focused and bringing me back to the original intent and mission of this book, multiple times. Surely you wearied of having to remind me repeatedly, but you never showed it. Though I still say I'm going to frame one sentence of a revision you sent me, so I don't forget it and because it makes me chuckle every time I think about it: "This is an example of too much detail with too little return." I think I could apply that to much of my life!

Thank you to our children, Matthew, Gabriel, Grace, and Anna, the unsung heroes, living a nomadic life for your growing up years and making so many sacrifices. You didn't get to choose that life, and I pray all the good times outweigh the difficult memories.

Thank you to Anna, Grace, Tyler, and Jeramae, for all your love and support during these last few challenging years.

Thank you to my parents, siblings, mother-in-law, and Papa Jack, now in heaven, for always being there and shoring us up through the years of military life. We love you.

And most of all, thank you to my favorite, my Steve, who continued to believe in and encourage me even when it didn't seem like this book would *ever* get finished. And *thank you* for your many years of faithful service to our country. You're my hero. And yes, I will go with you.

ENDNOTES

Part 1: Love Stories

1. "Military Spouse fact Sheet." U.S. Department of Labor. https://www.dol.gov/sites/dolgov/files/WB/mib/WB-MilSpouse-factsheet.pdf.

2. De Borja, Frederick M. "Divorce in the Philippines." De Borja Lamorena Duano and Navarro Law Offices. https://www.hg.org/legal-articles/divorce-in-the-philippines-a-legal-history-45701/.

3. "Alice Coffman." Veterans in Blue. https://www.veterans-in-blue.af.mil/Veterans/VetLib/Article/741539/alice-coffman/.

4. Ono, Hiromi, and Justin Berg. "Homogamy and Intermarriage of Japanese and Japanese Americans With Whites Surrounding World War II." Journal of Marriage and the Family, vol. 72, 5. October, 2010. https://www.ncbi.nlm.nih.gov/pmc/articles/PMC2992438/.

Part 2: Adventure Stories

1. Stilwell, Blake. "The Real-Life Murphy and how 'Murphy's Law' Came to Be." Military.com. https://www.military.com/history/real-life-murphy-and-how-murphys-law-came-be.html.

2. "What is the difference between a hurricane and a typhoon?" National Oceanic Atmospheric Administration. Last modified January 20, 2023. https://oceanservice.noaa.gov/facts/cyclone.html/.

3. "Super Typhoon status." National Weather Service. https://www.weather.gov/mfl/saffirsimpson/.

4. "Service Assessment: Super Typhoon Pogsona." U.S. Department of Commerce. April 2003. https://www.weather.gov/media/publications/assessments/Pongsona.pdf/.

5. Aydlett, Landon. "Weather Wednesdays: Super Typhoon Pongsona, 19 years later." *Pacific Daily News*. December 8, 2021. https://www.guampdn.com/news/weather-wednesday-super-typhoon-pongsona-19-years-later/article_e79ecdc2-56f9-11ec-8227-b76a292b64aa.html/.

6. "Military Family Lifestyle Survey, Comprehensive Report." Blue Star Families. https://bluestarfam.org/research/mfls-survey-release-2023/#reports/.

7. "S.1084—Military Spouse Licensing Relief Act of 2021." Congress.gov. https://www.congress.gov/bill/117th-congress/senate-bill/1084#:~:text=/.

8. "S.349—Military Spouse Employment Act of 2023." Congress.gov. https://www.congress.gov/bill/118th-congress/senate-bill/349/.

Part 3: Difficult Stories

1. Abdulle, Sahal. "Soldiers' corpses dragged through streets." Reuters. March 21, 2007. https://www.reuters.com/article/uk-somalia-conflict-idUKL2136851920070321

2. "Lorraine American Cemetery." American Battle Monuments Commission. https://www.abmc.gov/Lorraine/.

3. Musil, Donna. Pat Conroy as quoted in *Brats: Our Journey Home* (documentary), 2006. https://www.imdb.com/title/tt0487078/.

4. "Reunion and Reintegration." *Plan My Deployment.* Military OneSource. https://planmydeployment.militaryonesource.mil/reunion-reintegration/.

5. Brown, Brené. *Rising Strong: The Reckoning. The Rumble. The Revolution.* (New York: Random House Publishing Group, 2015), 180.

6. Lewis, C.S. *A Grief Observed* (New York: HarperOne, 2009), 15.

Part 4: Friendship Stories

1. Ehrenfeld, Temma. "To Age Well, You Need Friends," *Psychology Today* (blog), June 19, 2017. https://www.psychologytoday.com/us/blog/open-gently/201706/age-well-you-need-friends/.

2. Dickler, Jessica. "Military Families Face Financial Hurdles." *CNN: Money.* https://money.cnn.com/2012/03/27/pf/military-families/index.htm/.

3. Lieberman, E. James. "American Families and the Vietnam War," *Journal of Marriage and Family,* November 1971, https://www.jstor.org/stable/349445.

4. C.S. Lewis, *The Four Loves.* This quote is a composite drawn from two similar passages in this book. (New York: HarperOne, 2017) 83, 100).

5. Parker-Pope, Tara. "What Are Friends For? A Longer Life," *The New York Times,* April 20, 2009. https://www.nytimes.com/2009/04/21/health/21well.html.

Part 5: The Rest of the Story

1. Milzarski, Eric. "6 of the worst things to drink out of a grog bowl," *We Are the Mighty* (blog), October 30, 2020. https://www.wearethemighty.com/mighty-culture/worst-things-put-grog-bowl/.

MENTAL HEALTH AND COUNSELING

Confidential help from Military OneSource: Call toll-free 1-800-342-9647 or chat online at militaryonesource.mil/contact-us/.

Children and Youth Behavioral Military and Family Life Counselors from Military OneSource: part of the MFLC program above, specializing in children and youth. Online at militaryonesource.mil/non-medical-counseling/military-and-family-life-counseling/child-and-youth-behavioral-military-and-family-life-counselors/

Military and Family Life Counseling from Military One-Source: confidential, free non-medical counseling worldwide to service members, their families, and survivors. Online at militaryonesource.mil/non-medical-counseling/military-and-family-life-counseling/

Veterans Crisis Line: Dial 988 and press 1 or text 838255

ORGANIZATIONS AND WEBSITES

Blue Star Families: Founded to strengthen and empower military families. To that end, they are committed to groundbreaking research and committed partnerships, including keeping military families informed of the latest news and conducting yearly surveys. Online at bluestarfam.org

Bob Hope Village, Shalimar, Florida: An independent living community for Air Force widows in Shalimar, Florida, part of

Air Force Enlisted Village, funded by the Air Force Assistance Fund. Also part of AFEV: Hawthorn House, an assisted living and memory care residence. Online at afev.us

Comfort Crew for Military Kids: Support and resources with a vision to help military children thrive through the challenges and changes of military life. Online at comfortcrew.org.

Military Child Education Coalition: Programs and resources for military-connected children and their unique educational challenges. Online at militarychild.org

Military Family Books: Source for quality books for and about military family life. Online at militaryfamilybooks.com

Military Kids Connect: Resources for children as they go through military moves, deployments, and other transitions. Online at militarykidsconnect.health.mil

Military Spouse Advocacy Network: Network of advocates and mentors providing 24/7 peer-to-peer support, education, support, empowerment, and Leadership Development training to all military spouses. Online at militaryspouseadvocacynetwork.org

Mission: Milspouse: Originally called "Army Wife Network," M: M's mission is "to globally empower military spouses with resources and support them to conquer adversity, foster confidence, and thrive in this military life." Blog posts, podcast, and resources. Online at missionmilspouse.org

Operation We Are Here: An exhaustive list of resources and websites for the military community. Online at operationwearehere.com

The Submerged Life: The guide for Navy submarine spouses, written by submarine spouses. Online at thesubmergedlife.com

PUBLICATIONS AND PODCASTS

Be Safe, Love Mom by Elaine Lowry Brye. Help and support for parents of military members from a veteran spouse and mother of four active-duty members. (PublicAffairs, 2015)

Dispatches from the Cowgirl by Julie Tully. Part travelogue, part midlife coming-of-age memoir, enter the world of an American military spouse serving amongst the world's diplomatic corps, taking readers to the Africa Julie fell in love with and found hard to leave. (W. Brand Publishing, 2022)

Legacy **magazine:** A publication for service members, families, and their communities that operates from the premise that every individual is designed on purpose and for a purpose. Online at legacymagazine.org

MilitaryByOwner Advertising, Inc.: Buy, sell, or rent homes near military installations across the U.S. and its territories. Online at militarybyowner.com

Military Homeschool Podcast: With host Army wife Crystal Niehoff, it features topics relevant to military homeschooling families, interviews with experienced military homeschoolers and experts in education. Listen at ultimateradioshow.com/military-homeschool-podcast

Military Spouse **magazine:** The OG magazine for military spouses, "simplifying your crazy, wonderful military life." Online at militaryspouse.com

Milspouse Matters podcast with Jen McDonald. Since 2018, Jen has brought interviews with military spouses and military family experts along with practical tips and resources. Wherever you are in your military spouse journey, you'll find encouragement and help. Listen at jen-mcdonald.com/podcast/

Open When: Letters of Encouragement for Military Spouses by Lizann Lightfoot. A collection of letters for military spouses, offering encouraging words and practical advice throughout the journey of military life. (Elva Resa Publishing, 2021)

Seasons of My Military Student: Practical Ideas for Parents and Teachers by Stacy Allsbrook-Huisman and Amanda Trimillos. A guide for parents and teachers supporting military-connected students (Elva Resa Publishing, 2018)

The Meat and Potatoes of Life: My True Lit Com by Lisa Smith Molinari. Navy wife Lisa applies her wit and humor to marriage and military family life. Written in episodes, contained in seasons, her memoir is a sitcom for book lovers. (Elva Resa Publishing, 2020)

The Spouse Angle podcast. Hosted by Natalie Gross, bringing trusted, relevant news to military spouses and families. Listen at thespouseangle.com

You Are Not Alone: Encouragement for the Heart of a Military Spouse by Jen McDonald. Jen's first book of thirty daily readings and journal prompts designed to encourage, strengthen, and uplift military spouses through the unique challenges of military life. Written from the perspective of faith. (Little Things Press, 2016 and 2022)

FOR AFGHANISTAN ALLIES AND OTHERS

International Institute of St. Louis. Assistance for refugees and immigrants to secure jobs, housing, and healthcare. Online at https://www.iistl.org/

Keeping Our Promise. Comprehensive resettlement assistance to endangered wartime allies who served U.S. interests in conflict and war zones. Online at keepingourpromise.org

LIRS Connect. Largest faith-based nonprofit in the U.S. dedicated to immigrants, asylum seekers, and refugees. Founded in 1939. Online at lirsconnect.org

No One Left Behind. Dedicated to ensuring that America keeps its promise to U.S. interpreters and employees in Iraq and Afghanistan through the Special Immigrant Visa (SIV) programs. Online at nooneleft.org

Save Our Allies. Rescues and aids Americans and Allies in war-torn environments, resettles them as needed in environments free of tyranny and terror. Online at saveourallies.org

Save the Children: Ensuring children grow up healthy, educated, and safe in the U.S. and around the world, every day and in crisis situations. One mission is meeting urgent needs of immigrant and refugee children. Online at savethechildren.org

Women for Women. Emergency support for Afghan women and ongoing services in Afghanistan and other areas of conflict around the world. Online at womenforwomen.org

GLOSSARY OF MILITARY TERMS AND ACRONYMS

Explanation of some of the common military terms used in this book. Not a complete list!

AAFES, BX, NEX, MCEX, PX: Same thing, different service branches. AAFES: Army & Air Force Exchange Service; BX: Base Exchange; NEX: Navy Exchange; MCEX: Marine Corps Exchange; PX: Post Exchange. All mean the military's version of a department store located on the installation.

BAH, BAQ: Basic Allowance for Housing, Basic Allowance for Quarters. A monthly housing allowance for military members.

COLA: Cost of Living Allowance. Sometimes paid in addition to normal military allowances to offset expenses in overseas locations (Oversea COLA) or CONUS locations with higher cost of living.

CONUS, OCONUS: Continental United States, Outside the Continental United States. (Sometimes "contiguous" is also used). As with many military terms, this can be confusing, as CONUS means the lower 48 states. Overseas locations, Alaska, and Hawaii are all OCONUS.

DeCA, commissary: Defense Commissary Agency. The military's equivalent of a grocery store located on military installations worldwide.

DEERS: Defense Enrollment Eligibility Reporting System, the database of active duty and retired service members, their family members, and others who are eligible for TRICARE, the military's healthcare coverage.

DITY, PPM: Do-It-Yourself or Personally Procured Move. A move in which the military member either partially or fully administers a move, with reimbursement from the government later.

Duty Station or Assignment: Base or installation where military members work and live. Also, "stationed," i.e., "We were stationed in Germany."

ID card or ID: Issued by the military, your ID card is your key to access anything military related, including healthcare.

Leave: Time off. "I'm taking leave next week."

LES: Leave and Earnings Statement. A comprehensive statement of a military member's leave and earnings showing entitlements, deductions, allotments, leave information, and tax withholding information.

PCS: Permanent Change of Station, a military move. (And guess what? It's never permanent.)

Quarters: Buildings used to house military personnel.

Shoppette: The military's version of a convenience store, located on the installation.

Space-available flight: Space-A or "taking a hop," it allows authorized passengers to occupy Department of Defense (DoD) aircraft seats that are surplus. Space-A travel is free but allowed only if it doesn't interfere with mission needs.

SSN, SSAN or just "social": The military member's Social Security Number, their identifying number to the military for themselves and their dependents.

Related questions you'll hear:

- "Sponsor's social?" is shorthand for "What is your spouse's Social Security number?"
- "Last four?" is a request for the last four numbers of the SSN, usually your spouse's, not yours.

TDY/TAD: Temporary Duty Travel or Temporary Additional Duty. Travel or short-term assignment located away from the service member's permanent duty station.

TLF, lodging: Temporary Lodging Facility. Temporary quarters located on the installation.

VA: US Department of Veterans Affairs (encompasses Veteran's Health Administration and Veteran's Benefits Administration).

Other questions and phrases:

What's your sitrep?: This is an inquiry about your situational report, or update on current situation.

Yeah, I got your six/Watch your six: "I've got your back." Reportedly originated with WWI fighter pilots referencing behind the pilot as the six o'clock position.

Foam the runway (the polite definition): A path of fire extinguisher foam laid on a runway to assist aircraft in an emergency landing. Often said in other scenarios in terms of being prepared.

Comin' in hot: Ready to fire, ready to fight. Coming into a situation aggressively.

Semper Gumby: Always flexible.

SNAFU: "Situation normal, all f*cked up." Fun fact: this has now become a word in the dictionary with a definition fit for polite society, meaning a situation filled with errors and confusion.

Get comfortable being uncomfortable, hurry up and wait, the only easy day was yesterday: The meaning of these is clear. The military is full of phrases reminding us not to expect this life to be easy!

Different words for military installations

- Air Force, Navy, Marines: base (occasionally: station)
- Army: post, fort, camp

ABOUT THE AUTHOR

JEN McDONALD is a longtime writer and editor, the author of the Amazon best seller, *You Are Not Alone: Encouragement for the Heart of a Military Spouse* (Little Things Press, 2016), and the host of the *Milspouse Matters* podcast. She's been published in numerous national publications and books, including *Military Spouse* magazine, *Military.com*, and *Chicken Soup for the Soul: Devotional Stories for Tough Times* (Chicken Soup for the Soul, 2011), and has also been featured on national radio shows and podcasts. Jen was a military spouse for thirty years and is a mom to four young adults, including one son serving in the military. One of her happiest roles these days is being "Gigi" to her grandbabies. She and her Air Force husband, now retired, were stationed all around the world from Europe to the Pacific. Somewhere along the way—with a lot of practice—she learned to embrace the unknown. After decades of moving with the military, she is now planted in Texas. Jen loves to encourage and connect with other military spouses.

Find more from and about Jen, including her *Milspouse Matters* podcast, on her website: jen-mcdonald.com.

Connect with Jen on social media:

Facebook: @milspousematters and @jenmcdonaldwriter

Instagram: @milspousematters

Twitter: @jenmcdonald88 and @milspousematter